"Like Fire in Broom Straw"

Recent Titles in
Contributions in American History

The Frontier in the Colonial South: South Carolina Backcountry, 1736–1800
George Lloyd Johnson, Jr.

Keepers of the Spirits: The Judicial Response to Prohibition Enforcement in Florida, 1885–1935
John J. Guthrie, Jr.

Herbert Hoover and Franklin D. Roosevelt: A Documentary History
Timothy Walch and Dwight M. Miller, editors

Frontier Profit and Loss: The British Army and the Fur Traders, 1760–1764
Walter S. Dunn, Jr.

Socialism and Christianity in Early 20th Century America
Jacob H. Dorn, editor

The Final Frontiers, 1880–1930: Settling the Southern Bottomlands
John Solomon Otto

African America and Haiti: Emigration and Black Nationalism in the Nineteenth Century
Chris Dixon

A Chief Justice's Progress: John Marshall from Revolutionary Virginia to the Supreme Court
David Robarge

Keeping the Faith: Race, Politics, and Social Development in Jacksonville, Florida, 1940–1970
Abel A. Bartley

Members of the Regiment: Army Officers' Wives on the Western Frontier, 1865–1890
Michele J. Nacy

An Independent Woman: The Life of Lou Henry Hoover
Anne Beiser Allen

The American Dole: Unemployment Relief and the Welfare State in the Great Depression
Jeff Singleton

"Like Fire in Broom Straw"

Southern Journalism and the Textile Strikes of 1929–1931

Robert Weldon Whalen

Contributions in American History, Number 191
Jon L. Wakelyn, Series Editor

GREENWOOD PRESS
Westport, Connecticut • London

Library of Congress Cataloging-in-Publication Data

Whalen, Robert Weldon, 1950–
"Like fire in broom straw": Southern journalism and the textile strikes of 1929–1931 / by Robert Weldon Whalen.
p. cm.—(Contributions in American history, ISSN 0084-9219 ; no. 191)
Includes bibliographical references and index.
ISBN 0-313-31698-8 (alk. paper)
1. Journalism—Southern States—History—20th century. 2. American newspapers—Southern States. 3. Strikes and lockouts—Textile industry—Southern States—Press coverage. I. Title. II. Series.
PN4893.W48 2001
070.4'49331892877'0092275—dc21 00-052131

British Library Cataloguing in Publication Data is available.

Library of Congress Catalog Card Number: 00-052131
ISBN: 0-313-31698-8
ISSN: 0084-9219

First published in 2001

Greenwood Press, 88 Post Road West, Westport, CT 06881
An imprint of Greenwood Publishing Group, Inc.
www.greenwood.com

Printed in the United States of America

The paper used in this book complies with the Permanent Paper Standard issued by the National Information Standards Organization (Z39.48–1984).

10 9 8 7 6 5 4 3 2 1

Copyright Acknowledgments

The author and publisher gratefully acknowledge permission to reprint from the following:

Excerpts from the following are reprinted with permission of Rare Book, Manuscript, and Special Collections Library, Duke University, Durham, North Carolina:

Boyd Ellsworth Payton Papers

George Sinclair Mitchell Papers

J. Louis Engdahl, *Gastonia—A Class Case and a Class Verdict*. International Labor Defense flyer, undated.

"*Stand Behind the 23 Militant Gastonia Textile Workers*!" San Francisco Joint Defense and Relief Committee flyer, undated.

"*Marion—Food and Clothing for 175 Families Needed*!" Federal Council of Churches flyer, undated.

Excerpts from the following pamphlets are reprinted with permission of Special Collections Department, Southern Labor Archives, Georgia State University:

Paul Blanshard, *Labor in Southern Cotton Mills*.

Conference for Progressive Labor Action, *The Marion Murder*.

Sinclair Lewis, *Cheap and Contented Labor*.

Jesse Lloyd, *Gastonia*.

Myra Page, *Southern Cotton Mills and Labor*.

Excerpts from the following papers are reprinted with permission of the Southern Historical Collection, Wilson Library, The University of North Carolina at Chapel Hill:

Robert Cooke Papers

Frank Porter Graham Papers

Harriet Herring Papers

William Greene Raoul Papers

Excerpts from *Gaston County Centennial Brochure* (*1846–1946*). Gaston County Centennial Committee, undated. Reprinted with permission of Gaston County Public Library, Gastonia, North Carolina.

Excerpts from the following are reprinted with permission of McDowell County Library, Marion, North Carolina:

Debra Burleson, "The Strike of 1929 in McDowell County." Unpublished paper.

Cross Mill Records

Robin H. Hill Collection

Excerpts from the following are reprinted with permission of the Danville Public Library, Danville, Virginia:

Clippings, indexed by Clara G. Fountain

Dan River Mills File

Schoolfield File

Winding Through Time, Danville Bicentennial Committee Brochure, 1993.

Excerpts from the *Governor O. Max Gardner Papers* and the *Gertrude Weil Papers* are reprinted with permission of the North Carolina State Archives, Raleigh, North Carolina.

Every reasonable effort has been made to trace the owners of copyright materials in this book, but in some instances this has proven impossible. The author and publisher will be glad to receive information leading to more complete acknowledgments in subsequent printings of the book, and in the meantime extend their apologies for any omissions.

For my father, Weldon Smith Whalen,

and

in loving memory of my mother, Genevieve Casey Whalen

"Undeniably, there is a stir, a rustling upon the land, a vague, formless intangible thing which may or may not be the adumbration of coming upheaval. Tomorrow — the day after — eventually — the cotton mill peon will acquire the labor outlook and explosion will follow."

— W. J. Cash, "The Mind of the South" (1929)

"The facts we see depend on where we are placed and the habits of our eyes."

— Walter Lippmann, *Public Opinion* (1922)

Contents

Acknowledgments

This book was born of a complaint, a rejection, and lots of encouragement, and I am thankful for all three.

The complaint was mine. Trained as a German historian, I complained, several years ago, to my friend and colleague, Dr. Richard Rankin, about the difficulties of doing German history from the United States. Richard, a fine southern historian, suggested that I try my hand at American history. I have long been interested in American and southern history, and I thought I'd see where Richard's suggestions led.

They led to the industrial explosion of the early depression years, a powerful story that has only been partially told. I gathered vast amounts of compelling material, produced a vast, unwieldy, 900-plus page manuscript, and sent it off to a fine academic press. On the recommendation of an anonymous reviewer the press quite properly rejected the manuscript. But the reviewer did note that somewhere in that mountainous text there might be a good story about the southern press and its handling of the industrial turmoil, and that such a story might well be worth writing. That seemed like a remarkably good idea, and this book is the result.

And so I'd like to thank both Richard Rankin and that anonymous reviewer for their suggestions. Meanwhile, along the way, several dozen other people have encouraged me as I pursued this story, and I need to thank them as well.

Generous financial support for this research came in part from the Sam H. and Carolyn G. McMahon Jr. Professorship.

Dozens of librarians and archivists have helped, and I would like to thank them all, especially Rosemary Arneson, Lawrence Turner, and their colleagues at Everett Library at Queens College.

Let me thank too my colleagues in the history department at Queens College, William Thompson, Mollie Davis, Norris Preyer, Charles Reed, and Henry Kamerling, for years of good counsel.

The staff at Greenwood Press deserve a great deal of thanks, especially Heather Staines, and Marcia Goldstein. I owe particular thanks to Bobbie Goettler, my editor, for astonishing attention to detail and great patience with tardy authors. Without Bobbie's painstaking work, this little book would most likely never have been born. Thanks too to Professor Jon Wakelyn of Kent State University, the editor of this series.

My chiefest debt, however, is to Meg Freeman Whalen, pianist, musicologist, historian, and my best friend and soulmate, who took so much time from her own work to give to me. Thanks as well to our three children, James, Julia, and Cecilia; to Meg's surprise and mine, this book was completed before our children's retirement.

I've dedicated this book to my dad and to the memory of my mom. I hope it can be, in a very small way, public testimony to my thanks and love.

Abbreviations

AFL	American Federation of Labor
CN	*Charlotte News*
CO	*Charlotte Observer*
DR	*Danville Register*
DW	*Daily Worker*
ES	*Elizabethton Star*
GDG	*Gastonia Daily Gazette*
GDN	*Greensboro Daily News*
GR	*Greensboro Record*
GP	*Greensboro Patriot*
MT	*Mecklenburg Times*
MP	*Marion Progress*
NA	National Archives
NTWU	National Textile Workers Union
NYT	*New York Times*
RNO	*Raleigh News & Observer*
RNL	*Richmond News-Leader*
RT-D	*Richmond Times-Dispatch*
SHC-UNC-CH	Southern Historical Collection University of North Carolina at Chapel Hill
SOHP	Southern Oral History Project University of North Carolina at Chapel Hill
UTW	United Textile Workers

Introduction: "Like Fire in Broom Straw"

"Textile mill strikes flared up last week like fire in broom straw across the face of the industrial South," *Time* magazine's southern correspondent reported breathlessly in mid-April 1929.[1] *Time* was reporting on a wave of labor unrest that began that month in Elizabethton, Tennessee; crested later in Marion and Gastonia, North Carolina; and climaxed in January 1931, in Danville, Virginia.[2]

It was a bitter season. Writing from Marion, in October 1929, just after deputies had fired on a crowd of strikers, killing six of them, a *New York Times* reporter captured the region's grim mood: "An atmosphere of veritable civil war pervades this community, with sullen, embittered mill workers, many of them assembled in groups at street corners throughout the town, pitted against the rest of the community, which, with few exceptions, seems to be dead set against the union organizers and the mill workers' organizations." The reporter continued:

> [Labor union attorney D. F. Giles] impressed it upon Solicitor [J. Will] Pless that it would be in the interest not only of what the union considers justice but also of the public peace that some action be taken against the Sheriff and the others accused by the strikers if retaliatory moves on the part of the union men are to be avoided. Such actions, he said, might well mean the inauguration of a period of bloody guerrilla warfare against the officers of the law.[3]

After reporting for months on North Carolina's labor troubles, the *Times* editorialized: "Each new outrage . . . serves to reveal the extent of the social and economic warfare" raging in the Piedmont.[4]

Just weeks earlier, in September, after an explosion of vigilante violence, the *Greensboro Patriot* grimly warned:

> Where capital is willing to take an arbitrary stand, where labor is willing to take the law into its hands, there can be expected a warfare of bitter words and cowardly strife. Both these conditions exist in hundreds of southern manufacturing towns. Unless the state authorities can arrange a system of immediate and effective arbitration, and unless public sentiment is

trained to express the strongest condemnation for high-handed methods from either side, the south may be in for the bloodiest and bitterest commercial war on record.[5]

"You may sniff at the class struggle," Forrest Bailey wrote in *The New Republic*, "but whether you like it or not, here is the thing that the Communists call by that name — raw."[6] Reporter Anne O'Hare McCormick noted in 1930 that the strike wave "involved 17,000 workers and was characterized by savage violence, murders, kidnappings, evictions, military intervention everywhere and white-hot partisanship. There were no bystanders in this conflict; it had all the elements of class war."[7]

The strikes were one of the big stories of their day. Reporters from around the country hurried to the strike zone; labor activists from Mexico City to London to Berlin kept careful watch; the strikes inspired at least one play and six different novels.[8]

The strikes were symptoms of a profound crisis in the southern economy. Textiles had made the New South. The thousands of mills that had sprung up across the southern Piedmont in the decades after the Civil War wove the wealth that engendered the South's rebirth. Southerners looked on textiles with an almost religious reverence. Southern culture and politics were indelibly shaped by textile barons and mill village life. No industry had as profound an impact on the New South. Textiles were to the South, and especially the southern Piedmont, what steel was to Pittsburgh or automotives to Detroit.

In the mid-1920s, however, the South's textile industry was in deep trouble, and given the industry's centrality to southern life, these troubles had ramifications far beyond mill and market.

The strikes were a violent expression of the textile industry's long crisis. Beginning in March 1929, in Elizabethton, high up in the mountains of east Tennessee, where some 5,000 workers struck the German-owned Bemberg-Glanzstoff plants, strikes, protests, and walkouts flashed all across the southern Piedmont. In April workers trooped out of the massive Loray Mill in Gastonia, North Carolina. A score of flamboyant Yankee communists flocked to Gastonia and brought with them tribes of reporters. By the time the Gastonia strike was over, both the city's Police Chief and a woman striker would be shot to death. The trial of the strikers accused of killing the Police Chief, held in nearby Charlotte, was one of the great judicial dramas of the 1920s. By July 1929 workers in Marion, North Carolina, were off the job; six of them would be shot to death by deputies in October. Finally, in September 1930 workers in Danville, Virginia, launched a long and bitter strike against the huge Dan River company. These were only the most notable in a sea of industrial turmoil.

For southern reporters the strikes of 1929–31 were very big news. Front-page strike stories screamed from virtually every issue of the *Charlotte Observer*, the *Greensboro Daily News*, and the *Raleigh News &Observer,* while strike editorials boomed from inside.

The strikes, on the one hand, were hardly decisive. Workers were defeated again and again; millhands were driven back into the mills; unions never did take much root in the Piedmont; what few gains workers won were sunk almost immediately by the Great Depression, which overwhelmed the South just as the strikes were ending. It was, from the millhands' perspective, a pitiful business. As one *New York Times* reporter wrote: "Poverty, ignorance, and lack of opportunity . . . are the widespread manifestations of the [mill] system. The workers . . . are a hopeless lot and feel that they have little chance in any open struggle with the employers . . . almost invariably defeat is their lot." Many workers, the reporter thought, were "mountaineers," who were new to industry and defenseless before management.[9] Historian Dewey Grantham was right when he later wrote: "These spontaneous demonstrations accomplished little except to publicize the deplorable condition of southern workers."[10]

On the other hand, however, these strikes were part of an enormous tectonic shift in the southern mind, a tremendous reconfiguration in attitudes and values, in prejudices and aspirations, that would utterly transform the South by the end of the century. This transformation is just about the most dramatic thing to have occurred in the United States in recent times.[11] Its heroic moment was the civil rights movement of the 1950s and 1960s, but, as John Egerton has eloquently demonstrated, its origins go back much further, back to the embattled southern social reformers and trade unionists of the 1930s at least, and back to a fundamental reconsideration of southern verities that began at about the same time.[12]

In 1929, the year of the strikes, a brash young North Carolina journalist named Wilbur J. Cash finally worked up the courage to submit an article to H. L. Mencken's flashy magazine, *American Mercury*. Cash called his piece "Jehovah of the Tar Heels." It was a bitter satire, full of Menckenesque mockery, of North Carolina Senator Furnifold M. Simmons. Mencken loved it, published it in July 1929, and urged Cash to write more. That fall Cash submitted a second article, grandiosely called "The Mind of the South."[13]

Cash would spend the rest of his troubled life sorting out just what he meant by the "mind of the South." As his critics charge, he was often quite wrong. He was right about at least two things, however: there is a place that can rightly be called the South, and it does make sense to talk about the "mind" of the South — the values, attitudes, assumptions, prejudices, and hopes — of the people who live there. This book attempts to watch that mind at work. It assumes that one good place to do that, to see the southern mind fret and sort through problems and lie to itself, to see it change, is in the hometown papers that southerners, in places like Elizabethton and Marion and Gastonia and Charlotte and Raleigh and Danville, read over breakfast or talked about during lunch and dinner.

It is, to be sure, notoriously difficult to gauge a newspaper's influence. On the one hand, the South in the 1920s and 1930s was not much on reading. Illiteracy was widespread. North Carolina was one of the more progressive states in the South, but the 1920 census revealed that some 13.1 percent of all North Carolinians older than ten years old were illiterate. These numbers were even more striking when sorted into discrete categories. For example, of white North Carolinians older than ten, 8.2 percent were illiterate, but of black North Carolinians older than ten, 24.5 percent were illiterate. Of all adult North Carolinians (twenty-one and older), 16.9 percent were illiterate (10.7 percent of whites and 32.4 percent of blacks). Among rural adults twenty-one and older, 18.5 percent were illiterate (12.2 percent of whites and 34.7 percent of blacks). On a national scale of newspaper readership, North Carolina ranked forty-third of the forty-eight states. Only about one-third of the families in the state subscribed to a daily paper, which was low by national standards.[14]

You can read numbers in different ways, however. That one out of three North Carolina families subscribed to, and presumably read some of, and were almost certainly influenced by, a daily paper is a measure of the press's considerable influence even in a largely nonreading state. The *Charlotte Observer*'s circulation was nearly 47,000 in 1929, when Charlotte's population was 83,408. (Charlotte hosted as well, off and on, several rivals to the *Observer*, including the very popular *Charlotte News*.)[15] The *Raleigh News and Observer*'s circulation, posted proudly on the paper's front page, was around 40,000 in 1929, when the city of Raleigh's total population was only about 42,000. Altogether, North Carolina's daily newspapers circulated a total of 324,000 copies every day, at a time when the state's population was only around 2.5 million.[16] If these raw numbers are hardly decisive, they certainly demonstrate that lots of newspapers circulated day after day, year after year, everywhere throughout the state. There can be little doubt that southern newspapers, not just the big ones like the *Charlotte Observer*, the *Raleigh News and Observer*, and the *Richmond News-Leader*, but hometown papers like the *Elizabethton Star* and the *Gastonia Daily Gazette*, had an impact, and more likely than not a big impact, on southern opinion. The very concept of the "New South" was, after all, invented by newspaperman Henry Grady, and it was especially the newspapers that drove home the idea.

This book is about the way a small number of southern newspapers those most directly involved in reporting on the textile strikes — tried to comprehend and explain what was happening. Focusing on a small sample of papers permits an intensive rather than superficial reading. Likewise, concentrating on a single event, the strike wave of 1929–31, provides the opportunity to examine this journalism in some depth. The strike wave, though brief, was a time of intense emotion and social upheaval; it was one of those strange, revelatory moments in which, for a heartbeat, much that had been concealed was suddenly revealed.

Most books about newspapers focus on the often colorful lives of reporters and the turbulence of editorial politics. This book does not. For one thing, most editorials and many articles, especially in the smaller papers, were often unsigned, so it's next to impossible to determine which reporter wrote what. Besides, even if an article's author could be identified, biographical information about him or her often would be scarce. Were reporters required by their editors to report stories in certain ways? There's little evidence that they were, partly, to be sure, because so many records have disappeared. It does appear, though, that there was considerable informal cultural pressure to report certain things in certain ways. There was, in the 1920s, a distinctive southern journalistic culture. Papers were expected to play a specific role in southern society, and a reporter who didn't understand that role wouldn't be long employed. As powerful as these cultural expectations were, however, this book will argue that the journalism produced was neither homogeneous nor predictable.

More important, what really mattered were the stories and editorials themselves, not the reporters' biographies. This book treats the newspapers as texts to be interrogated, whose conscious and unconscious messages deserve careful examination. It attempts to trace the contours of journalistic discourse and is interested not in the journalists but the journalism.

This book tries to help us understand both the South and its journalism just a little better. To begin with, this book is a contribution to the ongoing, and, it seems, never-ending discussion of the many New Souths. One might well argue that there surely cannot be anything new said on this subject, but given its complexity and importance, there is indeed more to be learned about; for example, the representations of gender and class within the New South's class and caste society, and how those representations were disseminated by the media of the day, the hometown papers, and how hometown papers represented resistance to the structures of gender, class, and caste.

In taking the newspapers' stories about the 1929–31 strike wave as its theme, this book also adds to the rapidly expanding literature on southern labor. Long ignored and even despised, southern workers, especially millhands, have become the subject of an enormous, and frequently brilliant, literature. The strikes, despite their color and drama, are still only partially understood, however. (Gastonia has received great attention, Elizabethton relatively less, Marion and Danville none at all.) This book considers one crucial moment in the history of southern labor history from a distinctive and quite different vantage point.[17]

This book teaches, too, something about the press, and especially the southern press. Astonishingly enough, this is a subject few know very much about.

To be sure, there are rich, chatty, and anecdotal collections of reporters' memoirs, as well as several good centennial histories of individual newspapers, such as Jack Claiborne's *The Charlotte Observer: Its Time and Place, 1869–1986*. There are also biographies of several of the more famous editors, such as Henry Grady and Josephus and Jonathan Daniels. If one looks for careful studies of the southern press, of its role in southern life, of its characteristics and insights and prejudices, however, one finds little indeed. Aside from John Kneebone's fine *Southern Liberal Journalists and the Question of Race*,[18] constructed around the biographies of a half-dozen leading journalists, there is hardly anything else.

Studying stories is a tricky business. When you look at the ways reporters cover stories, the temptation is to assume there is some event that occurs quite on its own, has distinct features and is sometime later, reported. What you do then is compare the event to the report and see how well the latter conforms to the former. Did reporters get the story right?

This method is partly what needs to be done. There were, after all, real events — people really did strike, people really were killed. Reporters did try to describe, accurately and fairly for the most part, what happened.

But it's not that simple.

A moment's reflection demonstrates that separating "event" from "report" is tricky indeed. An event would not even survive in memory were it not reported by someone; indeed, what survives are not "events" at all but "reports" about events. It may be possible, through a judicious comparison of reports, to reconstruct something like an objective description of events, but it is essential to realize that events and reports about events are intimately tied.

Certainly since the 1960s, everyone has become acutely aware of the media's ability to shape the events they ostensibly so neutrally cover. From the media's eye shine a glowing, distorting, and blinding light. Flashing it on certain events and not others transforms the events illuminated and obscures those that aren't. Reporters, then, are like scientists whose very intervention in an experiment profoundly changes the dynamics of the system investigated.

The mental equipment reporters bring to bear, the metaphors they use, the vocabulary they deploy, pre-exists events. True, good reporters report what they perceive, but they do not perceive innocently. Their perceptions are to a large extent determined by their inherited and often unconscious conceptions about "reality." As Walter Lippmann wrote in 1922, "the facts we see depend on where we are placed and the habits of our eyes."[19]

Lest we collapse in solipsistic despair, we need to remember that events do retain some autonomy, and a reporter's collision with events may be jarring enough to force the reporter to question his or her own preconceptions. Reporters powerfully shape events, but events can force reporters to reshape themselves. One must ask "did the reporter get the story right?" But this question is at best only a beginning. A host of other questions immediately arise, questions about culture, about imagination, about the intersection of multiple realities, and these are some of the questions this book will examine.

The stories about the strikes, rather than the strikes themselves, are the focus of this book, because these stories reveal the southern mind at work. This book will examine the conscious dimensions of this mind — the arguments reporters and editorialists made about the events of their day, arguments transmitted to tens of thousands of their contemporaries. It will also investigate the unconscious dimensions of this mind — the metaphors and narratives built into, as it were, the very words the reporters used.

It matters how reporters tell their stories. On the eve of the southern strikes, Walter Lippmann and John Dewey had their famous long-distance debate about the nature of the press. Lippmann, in *The Public Opinion,* insisted on the need for expert reporters, people who could comprehend the vast amounts of information flowing in the modern world and interpret it for their fellow citizens. Lippmann envisioned a kind of two-tier media universe, with expert journalists at the top and their lay pupils on the bottom. Dewey, in *Experience and Nature* and elsewhere, worried about Lippmann-style experts, and argued that the press's chief responsibility was not to create experts but rather to nurture an informed and engaged citizenry. Dewey tended to think of reporters not as detached experts but as engaged citizens who collaborated with, and did not simply inform, their fellow citizens.

Three generations later the debate continues. Angry critics of the American media, such as James Fallows and others, insist like Dewey that the press's chief duty is to encourage and enhance democracy. They look for a kind of "public journalism" that is actively committed to democratic values. Their critics charge, though, that such "public journalists" too quickly lose sight of the kind of detached objectivity reporters are supposed to honor. Advocacy, without objectivity, too easily degenerates into propaganda. But then, what exactly is "objectivity"? Is a reporter who records, but does not intervene in, a murder, being an objective journalist or a moral monster? Are "objectivity" and "democratic advocacy" necessarily contradictory?[20]

For anyone interested in reporters and reporting, these matters are hardly news. What is new in this book is the attempt to see just how southern journalism wrestled with these issues and more as it attempted to describe and comprehend the traumatic events of 1929–31.

Late in 1929 North Carolina's Frank Porter Graham began collecting signatures for a resolution he intended to send to the newspapers. Frank Graham, a native North Carolinian, was the young and controversial faculty member and soon-to-be president of the University of North Carolina at Chapel Hill, and already, by 1929, he had made a name for himself as a southern reformer. Deeply disturbed by the troubles of that year, Graham had in mind a resolution by North Carolinians addressed to North Carolinians. Just a few days before Christmas, he wrote to Gertrude Weil, who, like Graham, had been involved in a wide variety of reform causes, and asked for her support. Graham explained that he already had the endorsement of President W. L. Poteat, of Wake Forest University; journalist Nell Battle Lewis; Charlotte's Methodist Bishop, Edwin Mouzon; sociologist Howard Odum; and many others. Weil added her name. By the time he was done, Graham would accumulate nearly five hundred signatures.

The resolution called for specific reforms in the textile industry; for a nationwide, nonpartisan scientific survey of the industry; and for recognition of the right of both capital and labor in the industry to organize and advocate their cause without restriction.

These three points rested on the resolution's first and most basic point, an unqualified reaffirmation of the fundamental rights of free speech and free assembly, "without regard to birthplace, race, ownership or labor status, unionism or non-unionism, religion, politics or economic views."

All four points were attempts to get at a central question, explained in the resolution's preamble: "In this time of economic transition and industrial struggle social attitudes are in process of formation critical with human meaning as to the sort of commonwealth we are to become.” The signatories, at the conclusion, explained that they wished to communicate to their fellow North Carolinians, “as citizens concerned with the building of this commonwealth.”[21]

The building of a commonwealth occurs first in people’s minds, in the “social attitudes” that are “in process of formation.” The debate about this particular commonwealth, the “rustling and stirring” and “adumbration of great upheaval,” which young Cash thought he heard, an adumbration somehow tied up with the rebellion of the millhands, was reflected and represented and fought out in the inky pages of the dozens of hometown papers, fought out messily between ads for Model-Ts, cranky letters to the editor, Betty Boop, and the sports page. It is this messy battle, which would mean so much in the end to so many, that this book will follow.

NOTES

1. “Labor — Southern Stirrings,” *Time*, April 15, 1929, 13.

2. Allen Tullos counts some 175 strikes in the Piedmont’s textile mills from the late 1920s to the mid-30s, Allen Tullos, *Habits of Industry* (Chapel Hill: University of North Carolina Press, 1989, 187–88. For a contemporary survey see also George Sinclair Mitchell, *Textile Unionism and the South* (Chapel Hill: University of North Carolina Press, 1931), especially Chapter III. The classic study of the 1929–31 textile strikes is Tom Tippett’s *When Southern Labor Stirs* (New York: Cape & Smith, 1931). Little has been written about Marion or Danville; about Elizabethton, see James Hodges, “Challenge to the New South: The Great Textile Strike in Elizabethton, Tennessee, 1929,” *Tennessee Historical Quarterly*, Vol. 23 (December 1964), 343–57; John Fred Holly, *Elizabethton, Tennessee, A Case Study of Southern Industrialization*, Ph.D. Dissertation, Clark University, 1949; and Jacquelyn Dowd Hall, “Disorderly Women: Gender and Labor Militancy in the Appalachian South,” *Journal of America History*, Vol. 73, No. 2, September 1986, 354–82. The best-known study of the Gastonia strike is Liston Pope, *Millhands and Preachers* (New Haven: Yale University Press, 1942); but see also John Salmond, *Gastonia 1929* (Chapel Hill: University of North Carolina Press, 1996). Few workers have been studied as thoroughly as the Southern millhands. For an introduction to this prodigious literature, see Robert Zieger, “Textile Workers and Historians,” in Robert Zieger (ed.), *Organized Labor in the Twentieth-Century South* (Knoxville: University of Tennessee Press, 1991).

3. “Marion Sheriff Held on Murder Charge,” *NYT*, October 4, 1929, 1.

4. “Rooted in the Soil” (editorial), *NYT*, September 20, 1929, 30.

5. “An Evil Portent” (editorial), *GP*, September 12, 1929, 4.

6. Forrest Bailey, “Gastonia Goes To Trial,” *The New Republic*, August 7, 1929, 332–34.

7. Anne O’Hare McCormick, “The South: The New Labor and the Old,” *NYT*, June 15, 1930, V, 8. No on really knows just how many millhands struck. Around 4,000 struck in Elizabethton; perhaps 2,000 in Gastonia; maybe another 2,000 in Marion; and again around 4,000 in Danville. Those were just the big strikes. Thousands of small strikes swept through the textile South especially in the spring and summer of 1929. John Salmond, in his account of the Gastonia strike, estimates, for instance, that in South Carolina alone some eighty-one

strikes involved 79,027 workers. See John Salmond, *Gastonia*, 9.

8. The novels are: Sherwood Anderson, *Beyond Desire* (New York: Horace Liveright, 1932); Fielding Burke (Olive Tilford Dargan), *Call Home the Heart* (New York: Feminist Press, 1983); Grace Lumpkin, *To Make My Bread* (New York: Macauley, 1932); Dorothy Myra Page, *Gathering Storm* (New York: International Publishers, 1932); William Rollins, *The Shadow Before* (New York: McBride, 1934); and Mary Heaton Vorse, *Strike*! (Urbana: University of Illinois, 1991). For more on the "proletarian novel" of the late 1920s and 1930s, see Daniel Aaron, *Writers on the Left* (New York: Columbia University Press, 1992); Ralph F. Bogardus and Fred Hobson, ed., *Literature at the Barricades: The American Writer in the 1930s* (Tuscaloosa: University of Alabama Press, 1982); and Walter B. Rideout, *The Radical Novel in the United States, 1900–1954* (New York: Columbia University Press, 1992). For a thorough study of the whole Popular Front culture of the thirties, see Michael Denning, *The Cultural Front* (New York: Verso, 1996).

9. "Again Gastonia Draws Eyes of the Nation," by Joseph Shaplen, September 29, 1929, *NYT*, X, 3.

10. Dewey Grantham, *The South in Modern America* (New York: Harper Collins, 1986), 161.

11. Heaven knows that there is no shortage of literature on the "New South." Labor's role in the transformations that characterized the New South is, though, a matter of considerable debate.

Both C. Vann Woodward, in *The Origins of the New South* (Baton Rouge: Louisiana State University Press, 1951) and Edward Ayers, in *The Promise of the New South* (New York: Oxford, 1992) discuss labor in general, and Ayers includes a chapter on "mill and mine," but neither portrays labor as playing a decisive role in the origins of the New South. George Tindall devotes two of his twenty chapters to labor in *The Emergence of the New South* (Baton Rouge: Louisiana State University Press, 1967), but they do not go beyond general descriptions of the labor turmoil of the 1920s. V. O. Key, in his famous *Southern Politics in State and Nation* (Knoxville: University of Tennessee Press, 1977) does not think that labor was of critical importance in Southern politics. The articles John Boyer and Evelyn Thomas Nolan collected in their historiographical anthology, *Interpreting Southern History* (Baton Rouge: Louisiana State University Press, 1987), devote little attention to labor. Larry Griffin and Don Doyle, in their *The South as an American Problem* (Athens: University of Georgia Press, 1995), do not see labor as a southern problem. Gavin Wright, in his *Old South, New South* (New York: Basic Books, 1986), does indeed discuss labor at length, but primarily as an economic factor. State histories, such as Hugh Talmage Lefler and Albert Ray Newsome, *North Carolina. The History of a Southern State*, third edition (Chapel Hill: University of North Carolina Press, 1973); William Powell, *North Carolina Through Four Centuries* (Chapel Hill: University of North Carolina Press, 1989); Louis D. Rubin, *Virginia. A History* (New York: Norton, 1984); Virginius Dabney, *Virginia* (New York: Doubleday, 1971); and Wilma Dykeman, *Tennessee. A Bicentennial History* (New York: Norton, 1975) typically devote, at most, a paragraph or two to the "labor troubles" of 1929-31. John Egerton, in *Speak Now Against the Day* (New York: Knopf, 1994), writes at length about the centrality of labor issues to southern progressives, but among the more general studies of southern life, Egerton's approach is unusual.

12. Edgerton writes that between, say, the election of Franklin Roosevelt in 1932 and the

end of World War II in 1945, "the South left Yesterday and entered Tomorrow." Egerton, *Speak Now*, 8.

13. "The Mind of the South," *American Mercury* XVII (1929), 310–18. See also his article specifically on the strikes, "The War in the South," *American Mercury*, XIX (1930), 163– 69. Both are reprinted in Joseph Morrison, *W. J. Cash: Southern Prophet* (New York: Knopf, 1967), and discussed both in Morrison and in Bruce Clayton, *W. J. Cash* (Baton Rouge: Louisiana University Press, 1991), 79ff.

The fantastic story of Cash's struggle to produce *The Mind of the South* has been told many times. Cash's first submission to Mencken was "Jehovah." After that Cash published five more articles with Mencken: "The Mind of the South" (1929); "The War in the South" (1930); "Close View of a Calvinist Lhasa" (1933) (a satire of Charlotte, North Carolina); "Buck Duke's University" (1933); "Holy Men Muff a Chance" (1934); and "Genesis of a Southern Cracker" (1935). Meantime, in 1929, Mencken had passed Cash's name along to publishers Alfred and Blanche Knopf (who shared offices with Mencken), and suggested that they might want Cash to do a book on the South. Blanche Knopf contacted Cash, who excitedly agreed. For the years, the Knopfs kept after Cash to write the book. It would finally appear in 1941.

14. Samuel Huntington Hobbs, *North Carolina: Economic and Social* (Chapel Hill: University of North Carolina Press, 1930), 266– 67; 272.

15. Hobbs, *North Carolina: Economic and Social*, 211; Claiborne, *The Charlotte Observer*, 195.

16. Hobbs, *North Carolina: Economic and Social*, 62.

17. The literature on the New South is far too voluminous to cite here. Among the classic discussions are: Ayers, *Promise*; Woodward, *Origins*; Tindall, *Emergence*; Majorie Spruill Wheeler, *New Women of the New South* (New York: Oxford University Press, 1993); I. A. Newby, *Plain Folk in the New South* (Baton Rouge: Louisiana State University Press, 1989); Paul M. Gaston, *The New South Creed* (New York: Vintage, 1973). Long neglected, southern labor is now a richly explored topic. Robert Zieger's article, "Textile Workers and Historians," in Zieger, *Organized Labor*, is the best introduction to the vast literature on the millhands and the textile industry. Broadus Mitchell's *The Rise of Cotton Mills in the South* (Baltimore: Johns Hopkins University Press, 1921), is usually cited as the first serious scholarly examination of the textile industry and its workers. George Sinclair Mitchell's *Textile Unionism and the South* (Chapel Hill: University of North Carolina Press, 1931) is one of the earliest studies of the trade-union movement in textiles. The basic narrative of the 1929–31 strikes is Tippett's *When Southern Labor Stirs*. Another useful early study of textile workers is: Herbert J. Lahne, *The Cotton Mill Worker* (New York: Farrar and Rinehart, 1944). Harriet Herring was a social worker affiliated with the University of North Carolina; her studies of millhands and mill villages are basic texts: *Welfare Work in Mill Villages* (Chapel Hill: University of North Carolina Press,1929); *Passing of the Mill Village* (Chapel Hill: University of North Carolina Press,1949). See also Marjorie Potwin's *Cotton Mill People of the Piedmont: A Study in Social Change* (New York: Columbia University Press, 1927). Beginning in the 1970s a series of fascinating social-historical studies of millhands and mill villages began to appear, including Melton McLaurin's *Paternalism and Protest: Southern Cotton Mill Workers and Organized Labor, 1875–1905* (Westport, Connecticut: Greenwood Press, 1971), and Dwight Billings' *Planters and the Making of a "New South": Class:*

Politics, and Development in North Carolina, 1865–1900 (Chapel Hill: University of North Carolina Press, 1979). By the 1980s historians had begun producing a series of powerful social-historical studies. They include such well-known works as David Carlton, *Mill and Town in South Carolina,1880–1920* (Baton Rouge: Louisiana State University Press, 1982); Jacquelyn Dowd Hall et al., *Like a Family* (Chapel Hill: University of North Carolina Press, 1987); Cathy L. McHugh, *Mill Family: The Labor System in the Southern Cotton Textile Industry, 1880–1915* (New York: Oxford University Press,1988); Allen Tullos, *Habits of Industry: White Culture and the Transformation of the Carolina Piedmont* (Chapel Hill: University of North Carolina Press, 1989); Douglas Flamming, *Creating the Modern South. Millhands and Managers in Dalton, Georgia, 1884–1984* (Chapel Hill: University of North Carolina Press, 1992).

18. Claiborne, *Charlotte Observer*. John Kneebone, *Southern Liberal Journalists and the Question of Race, 1920–1944* (Chapel Hill: University of North Carolina Press, 1986).

19. Walter Lippmann, cited in Herbert Gans, *Deciding What's News* (New York: Vintage, 1980) 310.

20. See James Fallows, *Breaking News: How the Media Undermine American Democracy* (New York: Vintage, 1997) 238–44.

21. See Warren Ashby, *Frank Porter Graham, Southern Liberal* (Winston-Salem: Blair, 1980). Letter from Frank Porter Graham to Gertrude Weil, December 22, 1929; Letter from Frank Porter Graham to Gertrude Weil, January 30, 1929, Gertrude Weil Papers, General Correspondence, 1929–32, North Carolina State Archives.

1

Eruption and Astonishment

In October 1928 presidential candidate Herbert Hoover's campaign train chugged through the soaring mountains around Elizabethton, Tennessee, and Mr. Hoover himself stopped by to visit.

Elizabethton and nearby Happy Valley are perched high up in the breathtaking mountains that straddle western North Carolina and eastern Tennessee. The mountains are huge, wooded, brooding, and spectacular, and Mr. Hoover must have been impressed by the scenery. But the citizens of Elizabethton had something almost as amazing as their mountains to show him.

That fall Elizabethton's spanking new Bemberg and Glanzstoff Corporation textile factories were in full operation, under the direction of Dr. Adolf Mothwurf.[1] Every day, close to 5,000 people passed through their gates, making them just about the biggest thing not just in Elizabethton, but in all of East Tennessee.

And so, in the fall of 1928, Elizabethton's community leaders cheerfully led Mr. Hoover through their new plants, and presented him with a sample suit of underwear.[2] In a pleasant speech Mr. Hoover praised the blessings of commerce and congratulated the citizens of Elizabethton on their shiny new factories.[3]

No one was prouder of those factories than the *Elizabethton Star*.[4] *The Star* was Elizabethton's only paper and it was the little city's most enthusiastic booster. *The Star* loved to call Elizabethton the "city of power" and the "wonder city," and there was no denying that in early 1929, Elizabethon was in the midst of a grand boom.

On Tuesday, January 1, 1929, the *Star*'s editorial confidently predicted a good year for business. The outlook, the editorial explained, was "more optimistic . . . than at any previous time." Business would do well, and "when big business moves ahead, there are jobs for all!" American Glanzstoff had just offered a new stock issue and, the *Star* predicted, Elizabethton might be getting yet another factory. A new hotel was being built, "hundreds of new homes" were underway, the First Baptist Church was nearly finished, and, the paper excitedly concluded, population was sure to grow maybe even to 10,000![5] Of course, there'd be serious competition from arch-rival Johnson City, but, the *Star* predicted, Elizabethton was sure to prevail.[6]

Not everyone would be impressed with Elizabethton and its factories. Novelist Sherwood Anderson hurried to the city in the spring of 1929 when the strike began and looked at Elizabethton with a jaundiced eye. He was, on the one hand, deeply impressed by the giant Bemberg-Glanzstoff mills. "The mills themselves," he wrote, "had that combination of the terrible with the magnificent that is so disconcerting. Anyone working in these places must feel their power." As for the city, Anderson thought Elizabethton "neither very beautiful nor very ugly." Yes, the city was growing; in 1920 Elizabethton had a mere 2,749 citizens, he reported, and by 1929 had over 8,000. Much of the town was, in fact, less than five years old, and the hastily constructed buildings, Anderson thought, already had "that half-decrepit worn-out look that makes so many American towns such disheartening places. There is a sense of cheapness, hurry, no care for the buildings."[7]

The *Star*, of course, couldn't have disagreed more. "Greatness of South Looms as Inevitable," the *Star* cheered in an article in January that discussed industrial development in the old Confederacy. Bemberg-Glanzstoff's director, Dr. Mothwurf, confidently told the paper that the Glanzstoff plant would hire an additional 1,200 workers, bringing the total Bemberg-Glanzstoff workforce to around 5,000. "We hope to practically double the volume of production of the American Glanzstoff Corporation," Mothwurf told the *Star* at the end of January.[8]

Bemberg-Glanzstoff officials not only promised new jobs, but also explained that they were eager to guarantee the happiness of their current employees. A new company magazine would soon appear, one that would, company officials said, "bring about a closer co-operation between employer and employes." The Bemberg company band announced a concert for early February, to be held in the Junior High auditorium. The evening would include showing a film made of President Hoover's visit to Elizabethton the previous fall.[9] Meanwhile, the Bemberg-Glanzstoff Club was under construction. It would include tennis courts, golf links, a swimming pool, a fine club-house, and provide recreation for the corporations' hard-working executives and the local business elite.[10] Bemberg-Glanzstoff was also the indirect owner of the Watauga Development Corporation, a real-estate firm that owned some 2,000 acres in nearby Happy Valley. Watauga announced a plan to build up to 1,000 homes that could be sold to Bemberg-Glanzstoff employees. The *Star* was enthusiastic about the housing plan and assured its readers: "It is something new to industrial workers in the south, who work for large corporations, to get this kind of treatment. It will be appreciated and will be mutually beneficial in the long run to both the companies and the employes."[11]

The *Star* just couldn't restrain itself as the mountain winter gave way at last to mountain spring. "No citizen of Elizabethton could fail to have just pride at the rapid development in progress here," said one editorial. "One can scarcely go into any part of Elizabethton and look in any direction without seeing new construction. . . . Elizabethton is beginning to arrive."[12] A week later the paper boasted that Elizabethton "combines all that is ideal for those who seek opportunities. Elizabethton will one day be one of the largest cities of the South."[13] Economic prosperity, the *Star* explained, ought to be the top priority of every citizen, and Elizabethton was lucky to have a prosperous corporate citizen like Bemberg-Glanzstoff.[14]

The *Elizabethton Star*'s enthusiasm in 1929 was not simply the product of optimistic editors. In that enthusiasm you could hear the voices of generations of reporters long since gone to glory. The voice of the southern press had been decisively shaped in the late nineteenth century by Henry Grady and the other creators of the New South. The southern press's vocabulary, its stock of recurring metaphors, the most fundamental terms of its discourse, were not created anew by each paper each day, but rather were transmitted, from paper to paper, from decade to decade. In its booming and boasting, the *Star* was utterly generic. Its articles and editorials were as much incantations as journalistic creations; they were ritual repetitions of communal beliefs forged long ago. In fact, there was hardly a southern newspaper that didn't sound exactly like the *Elizabethton Star*.

Listen, for instance, to the *Charlotte Observer*. Charlotte in 1929 was what Elizabethton hoped one day to become. "Charlotte, North Carolina," Louis Stark wrote for *The New Republic*, "is a busy, thriving city. The streets are bustling with activity. Hotels are crowded with tourists and traveling salesmen. From their offices in the city, mill executives direct a network of operations covering the state."[15]

In May 1929, despite the brutal class war swirling around it, an *Observer* editorial called "The Mighty South," boasted of the South's roaring economy.[16] In early June the *Observer* reported that the Federal Reserve Bank in Richmond had recorded a significant up-tick in the southern Piedmont's business over the year before. Other *Observer* stories that June continued the panegyric to capital. "Piedmont Trade and Industry Flourish" trumpeted the *Observer* on its front page on Saturday, June 1. Reporting on the growth of industry in the South, the *Observer* called a later story, "A Tale of Growth Beyond Equal: Romantic Story of North Carolina's Industrial Growth from Small Beginnings." The report was filled with superlatives: "unparalleled growth," "marvelous development," a "tremendous" story. The *Observer* announced in another story at the end of the month that it would publish its annual "tabloid magazine" recording the "developments and advantages" of textile manufacture in the South. And Charlotte, the *Observer* boasted, with some 750 cotton mills and 100 hosiery mills within a 75-mile radius, was the center, the hub, the omphalos of southern textiles.[17]

All this is what Paul Gaston has described as the "New South Creed."[18] It is a kind of mythology, a rich treasury of images and epithets that, like any myth, not only tries to impress meaning on chaotic reality, but also tries to keep the contradictions and paradoxes of life united in a kind of emotional and intellectual poetic conceit.

The New South Creed that governed the discourse of the *Star*, the *Observer,* and virtually every other newspaper in the South in the 1920s, had two parts. The first part was an unshakable allegiance to entrepreneurial capitalism. The New South Creed was the self-image of an optimistic, deal-making, endlessly promoting business class. Its hero is most certainly not the languid plantation aristocrat, surrounded by slaves, but rather the snappy businessman, all hustle and promise.

The second part of the creed was, ironically, nostalgia for the Lost Cause. Ritual defense of The Lost Cause — the obsessive praise for the heroic Confederacy — was both therapeutic and functional. The Lost Cause had first emerged as a coherent set of myths and rituals in the aftermath of the South's defeat and occupation, and it obviously served the therapeutic purpose of infusing meaning into the war and obscuring the defeat. The Lost Cause mythology was functional as well, however. At its heart was the historically dubious but endlessly asserted claim that all white southerners, despite class, had rallied to the Confederacy. Like all species of nationalist-myth, the Lost Cause defused class tension by appealing to racial solidarity, solidarity constructed around emotionally charged myths and rituals. One way for the New South to avoid class conflict was to fetishize white solidarity and white supremacy.

The Lost Cause also made radical change palpable by reaffirming the old verities at the very time that the New South was hurrying to transform them.

To be sure, progress and nostalgia are contraries; keeping new South boosterism and Lost Cause nostalgia in peaceful orbits around each other was the task of the South's press. The Charlotte papers, the *Charlotte Observer*, the *Charlotte News*, and the county paper, the *Mecklenburg Times*, provide classic illustrations of what inventive journalists could do.

In June 1929 the Confederate army rallied in Charlotte. Charlotte was the host of the Thirty-ninth annual reunion of the Confederate Veterans, and as the great date neared, Charlotte papers were filled with stories about the "Lost Cause," and "Lee and Jackson" and the "Southern Heritage." Charlotte expected thousands of guests for the event. The governor was coming; trainloads of elderly veterans, the Sons of Confederate Veterans, and the Daughters of Confederate Veterans were all scheduled to descend on the Queen City.[19] The churches, the Boy Scouts and Girl Scouts, all the city's philanthropic and fraternal organizations, all turned out to host the big event.

The best guess was that some 4,500 Confederate veterans attended the reunion, together with at least 50,000 family members and guests. They arrived on Sunday, June 2, and stayed the week. The big parade was on Friday, June 7, and on that day, wave on wave of old men marched through downtown Charlotte, surrounded by a sea of rebel flags. The papers were full of Confederate nostalgia. The whole affair, the *Charlotte News* predicted in its best boomer voice, would attract "the greatest crowd of visitors ever assembled on the streets of Charlotte."[20] The reunion was, of course, a "great honor for the State and for Charlotte," said the *Mecklenburg Times*; "there has never before been such an occasion in Charlotte. There may never be again."[21] There were dozens of speeches. North Carolina Governor Max Gardner welcomed the veterans. Mississippi Senator Pat Harrison explained that slavery had had nothing to do with the war, that the real issues had been states' rights and self-defense against the northern invasion of the South.[22]

That month Charles Morrow Wilson published an article in a national magazine, *The Outlook*, called "The Contradictory South." The editors of the *Mecklenburg Times* were impressed, and reviewed the article for their readers. Wilson, said the *Times*, "points out that this section is old-fashioned and with traditions, it is primitive and backward, it is also ultra-modern and progressive, cultured and crude, bigoted and yet broad-minded."[23]

In fact, the juxtaposition of progress and nostalgia, far from being contradictory, was, the *Charlotte Observer* argued, touching and poignant. An *Observer* reporter captured this mythic assertion in a striking anecdote:

> Two gray-haired men stood on the corner of Trade and Tryon streets yesterday, unmindful of the swirling traffic about them. As they lifted their eyes toward the bank building with its wealth of Confederate flags and buntings decorating the entire outer surface, they did not notice the harsh honk of auto horns, the press of hundreds of busy people, or the bustle of uptown trade. "My, but they look good," said one of the men, slightly older than his companion. He shaded his eyes as he looked at the row of bright-hued battle flags of the Confederacy. "Just like they flew 'em in the war," said the other. They stood on the curb while scores of persons passed by. Two girls of the flapper age stared at them curiously. . . . A young collegian, hatless and hurrying, almost bumped into them.[24]

It is a perfect piece. It is more than anecdote, it is epiphany. The old veterans surrounded by swirling traffic; the bank decorated with Confederate bunting; the hatless young collegian almost bumping into the aged soldiers; above all, the benediction by the veterans: "my but they look good . . ." all show that the magic worked, that the myths of the New South and the Lost Cause still held themselves, and the South, together.

The southern press's frontiers of discourse had been marked decades before, and African Americans, poor whites, and millhands lived beyond those frontiers. When one or another burst across the frontier, when for example, thousands of striking millhands flooded the streets in protest, the press responded with astonishment.

In the second week of March 1929, a young woman named Margaret Bowen, a section chief in the inspection room in the Glanzstoff plant in Elizabethton, went to her foreman to ask for a raise for herself and her section. Instead of a raise, she was demoted and her pay was cut.[25]

On March 12, 1929, all but seventeen of the 360 inspection room women who worked with Bowen walked off the job. The women milled around the factory and intercepted both the outgoing and incoming shifts. Almost immediately trouble broke out. Rumors swept the plant that one of the security guards, Buck Little, had hit one of the "girls" with a blackjack. A male worker rushed Little and hit him on the head with a lead pipe. Other groups of workers started throwing rocks at the security police. Dr. Mothwurf rushed out to see what was happening and a flying rock hit him on the head.[26] The Elizabethton strike established a ritual that would become painfully familiar throughout the Piedmont. Workers walk off the job and demand a host of reforms; management showers the strikers with injunctions obtained from friendly judges, and quickly convinces state politicians to rush in the National Guard; workers scramble to maintain picket lines as management, defended by the "special deputies" and the National Guard, ruptures the picket lines to bring in scabs; workers struggle to mobilize public opinion and keep their own spirits up with rallies and marches; in the end, management evicts the workers from their company-owned homes, starves them out, shatters the union, and the strikes collapse.

And through it all, the press would tell the story, amazed.

The *Elizabethton Star*, for example, hadn't a clue that there was any trouble brewing in the Bemberg-Glanzstoff mills. It viewed the strikes with dismay. In a March 15 editorial, the *Star* wrote:

> Strikes always cause trouble. . . . The people of Carter County have been almost universally loyal to the success of the large industries. The people of Carter County want prosperity and industries in operation. . . . The ideal toward which all fair-minded people look is a contented, satisfied population, satisfied and happy. Let us hope that the strike will be settled and that there will be no more labor troubles in this vicinity.[27]

There is nothing in the paper in the months before the strike even suggesting worker dissatisfaction. When the strike erupted the *Star* reported it fairly enough, but with a kind of stunned spectator's detachment.

Reporting an early rally, the *Star* noted that the air vibrated with shouts and calls, all, though, "more hilarious than angry." By noon that chilly spring day, downtown Elizabethton was filled with workers. "Hundreds of girls rode through Elk Avenue," the paper reported; they were on their way to a rally at the Carter County auditorium "in busses and taxis, shouting and laughing at people who watched them from the windows and store-fronts." [28] On March 21 another parade of workers poured down Elk Avenue, some workers walking along, others riding in trucks and cars, all of them shouting and singing. Only a few years before, there had been a violent textile strike, up north, in Passaic, New Jersey, and the sights the *Star* saw had a New Jersey feel to them. "Elk Avenue," the *Star* reported,

> seemed today to be transformed into one of the main streets of Passaic, N.J. as similar scenes to those enacted during the prolonged strike in that city were re-enacted in Elizabethton. Hundreds of workers milled about the streets. . . . Trucks, filled with young girls and boys, threaded their ways in and out of the normal traffic, the workers shouting as though they were enroute to a picnic instead of participants in a strike.

Strikers, the *Star* said, waved banners and American flags and bantered with the crowds who formed along the street.[29]

The National Guard rushed in; the labor dispute was quickly militarized, and the community polarized. A tentative settlement was reached on March 22, only to be broken by management even before the ink was dry.[30] Early in April vigilantes, central characters in the long textile crisis, appeared. Deep in the night of April 3, hooded gunmen kidnapped the organizer from the United Textile Workers, Al Hoffmann, and his colleague, Ed McGrady. The gunmen warned both never to return.[31] On Friday, April 5, however, Hoffmann and McGrady made a triumphant return to Elizabethton, surrounded by dozens of millhands all armed to the teeth. Packed in a long convoy of cars, the workers cruised slowly through Elizabethton's streets, shouting defiance at the vigilantes. A *New York Times* reporter wired: "[Hoffmann and McGrady], escorted by two score union workers, among them many girls in automobiles . . . paraded through the streets."[32]

The kidnapping affair flashed national light on Elizabethton. William Green, the president of the American Federation of Labor, rushed to Elizabethton, spoke to the strikers, and denounced the vigilantes.[33]

The strike, ostensibly settled on March 22, erupted again in mid-April and dragged on for several weeks more. Hugh Kerwin, head of the federal Labor Department's Conciliation Service, spoke by telephone with union organizer Al Hoffmann on the morning of April 16.

"How are things down there?" Kerwin asked.

"On Friday," Hoffmann responded, "two union boys were fired at the Glanzstoff. Grievance committee objected, and the company would not put them back . . . the committee of employees and the two boys were all fired . . . the workers got together . . . and appointed a committee of four . . . they endeavored to reach the management [from] 8 o'clock on Monday until 4 o'clock in the afternoon. They telephoned every half hour. Dr. Mothwurf . . . refused to talk with them. . . . The people just walked out. A complete walkout, 5,500 workers of both plants. . . . The people simply got tired of the actions of the company and they have just revolted and walked out on them. . . . They are trying to get scabs. I cannot tell what time something may happen. If they stay shut down, trouble may be avoided but if they start up there will be trouble. They have just revolted and came out on their own.[34]

Over the next few weeks, the *Star* faithfully chronicled what happened. Hundreds of strikers were arrested by police and National Guardsmen, and their hastily conducted trials became gaudy pantomimes.

Heavily armed National Guard troops surrounded the Carter County Courthouse. Platoons of defendants and their supporters hooted and booed as prosecutors tried to make their case, and they laughed with derision at judges' attempts to gavel them into silence. The audience "were loud in their approval of the 'smart' and flippant answers given on cross examination by some of the girl witnesses." At one point, the United Textile Workers' Bill Kelly, "vaulted the rail to the space in front of the judges and made a short impassioned talk, urging the union members to be quiet and observe court regulations. The disturbance then subsided. In a surprise move, union lawyers swore out an arrest warrant for Tennessee Attorney General Boyd himself, charging that his orders to the National Guard had led to the near death of one striker."[35]

April passed into May and still there was no reconciliation. Major George Berry, president of the International Pressmen's Union, appointed by Tennessee Governor Henry Horton to work as mediator, was convinced that Bemberg-Glanzstoff simply wouldn't budge. Furious at the steady increase in the number of National Guardsmen, he quit in disgust, telling reporters that "it is quite apparent that the concerns at Elizabethton do not desire to settle by mediation but desire to settle by force."[36]

The strike finally ended on May 26, with a rough compromise arranged by federal arbitrator Anna Weinstock. Many outsiders at first thought the deal a worker victory.[37] It wasn't. Strikers were supposed to be rehired; most weren't. Promised pay raises never materialized. Management imposed a rigid censorship on the shop floor and set up a company union.[38]

Complaints soon flooded the Labor Department in Washington. Someone sent in a flyer that management had circulated among its employees. It said: "Friendly Advice! Keep your money to yourself. Do not give assistance to those seeking to create discord between you and your employers. If you do you may destroy the source on which you depend for a living. Your success with this company will, under all circumstances remain purely a question of your COOPERATIVE relation to the Management."[39]

All through the summer of 1929, observers, including federal mediator Weinstock, warned of a renewed worker rebellion.[40] Weinstock laid the blame for the continuing troubles on management's recalcitrance.[41] In September 1929 J. Clyde Donnelly, President of Local 1630 of the UTW, and Margaret Bowen, the Local's secretary, wrote to Hugh Kerwin, director of the federal mediator service. They warned that "conditions in Elizabethton . . . are very serious with grave danger of a strike" and denounced management's bad faith.[42]

Trouble continued in Elizabethton well into the spring of 1930.[43] Sheriff J. M. Moreland surprised everyone by resigning in protest, refusing to use force against what remained of the union. "I was forced out," he told reporters, "by a bunch that wanted me to go out on the highways and shoot down pickets if they didn't do like these people wanted them to do."[44] There was no doubt that by the spring of 1930, however, that the union was quite dead in Elizabethton. There were still some small protests,[45] and an occasional bomb scare,[46] but as union activist Tom Tippett would write, all that was left of the jubilant unionism of 1929 were "a few hundred unemployed ex-strikers, half-starved and disillusioned, cynical and justly bitter."[47]

The *Elizabethton Star* was witness to all this, but strangely oblivious to much of it. The Star faithfully and accurately recorded the explosions and shootings and arrests that became so common in Elizabethton. Indeed, the *Star* was insistent on its "objectivity" and "non-partisanship" and many agreed that the *Star* really was being fair. On May 13, 1929, the *Star* published on its front page letters from Dr.

Mothwurf; Paul Aymon, President of the Tennessee State Federation of Labor; Bill Kelly, Vice-President of the United Textile Workers; and S. C. Rhea, president of the nonstriking "loyal workers" of Bemberg-Glanzstoff; and all testified to the paper's objectivity.

Throughout the strike season newspapers' "objectivity" would be the subject of constant public debate. In fact, it is well worth noting that most of the papers that reported on the strikes clearly made an attempt to "get the story straight." The *Charlotte Observer* published verbatim long reems of testimony during the trial of the Gastonia Seven. The *Danville Register* faithfully printed texts of company press releases and union leaders' speeches during the trouble in Danville at the end of the strike wave.[48]

The oddity was, however, that these quite accurate reports in the *Star* and elsewhere were structurally the same as the paper's regular reports on the random and context-less accidents and crimes and miscellaneous mayhem that were the stuff of every American newspaper. Reading these reports, readers would encounter a chaotic universe in which dangerous things happened, it seemed, for no reason and without any coherent context. Or rather, if there were a context, it was not that of social conflict and working-class rebellion, but that of random crime.[49] And that, in fact, was precisely a central message the *Star* wished to convey.

Strikes were not struggles for social justice. They were outbreaks of frightening crime. This was a consistent theme of the Piedmont's press and politicians. In a front-page editorial of May 13, the *Star* grimly warned of the "criminal outbreaks" sweeping through the city. To be sure, the *Star* evenhandedly defended both capital's right to a "fair and reasonable return on its investments," and labor's right "to seek, by any honorable and peaceful means betterment of . . . wage and working conditions." But, the paper insisted, labor-management conflict was not the real issue; "these . . . are entirely beside the real and vital issue before us." And the "real and vital issue" was the restoration of order. The absolute top priority was the re-establishment of authority. The editorial warned in the gravest terms of "acts of destruction" and "lawlessness." In the face of such a crime wave, the *Star* insisted, all disputes between labor and management should be postponed; "it is time," the *Star* argued, "for every right-thinking and God-fearing man and woman to band together in a common cause for the purpose of meeting this grave issue." Elizabethton and Carter County faced nothing less than a "reign of terror;" it was the "gravest challenge" this part of the world had faced in a century and a half.[50]

North Carolina's Governor, O. Max Gardner, said much the same thing. In late September 1929, Governor Gardner insisted that "questions of the stretch-out, communism and all other questions raised can be settled in the calm light of reason, but when the fabric of the law is weakened all other evils flow from it. . . . The situation in the state now only involves the supremacy of the law, and it shall be kept supreme."[51]

There was more than a hint of incipient hysteria in some of the *Star*'s reporting. When reporters learned the notorious communist, Fred Beal, who was leading the strike down in Gastonia, North Carolina, had come up to Elizabethton in May to make street-corner speeches, the *Star* described his visit as the beginning of a "Red Invasion."[52]

But through it all, what is significant about the *Star*'s reporting during the crisis is the paper's unshakable faithfulness to the obligatory optimism of the new South Creed. Although the paper's cheery tone took on an increasingly surreal quality in light of the chaos in the streets, the paper's mood rarely varied. Again and again, usually incorrectly, the *Star* insisted that "talks were very near."[53] And even in the midst of the crisis the paper returned obsessively to its old themes. Early in April, just after the kidnappings, the *Star* happily expressed a "new optimism" about Elizabethton's future. Montgomery Ward would soon be opening a store; Dr. Mothwurf promised to expand the Glanzstoff operation; the General Carter Hotel would soon be finished; the Chamber of Commerce talked about setting up a "welcoming committee" to recruit more industry for the city.[54]

Trapped in categories forged a half-century before, terrified by authority's breakdown, the *Star* clung to what it knew best, booming and boasting and cheerleading, even when such optimism was increasingly distant from what the paper could see with its very own eyes.

But this is not the whole story. The *Star*'s insistence on the accuracy of its reporting, for example, demonstrated that the *Star*, at least rhetorically, held to an ideal of reporting that stressed "getting the story right," and not merely ideological conformity. More important, the *Star*'s claim to be above the fray, while transparently false, was also of considerable importance. Most often, the *Star* was an advocate of capital, or rather, of specific interests, those of the Bemberg-Glanzstoff corporation. The *Star* claimed, however, to represent not simply certain interests but the people at large; not only capital but the wider commonwealth. Still murky with the besieged *Star*, this way of thinking about journalism, this argument that journalism ought to represent not merely wealth but the commonwealth, would have important consequences as the great textile crisis continued.

NOTES

1. For overviews of the Elizabethton Strike, see Philip Foner, *History of the Labor Movement in the United States*, Volume 10 (New York: International Publishers, 1994), 275; Jacquelyn Dowd Hall, "Disorderly Women: Gender and Labor Militancy in the Appalachian South," *The Journal of American History*, Vol. 73, No. 2, September 1986, 354–82; James A. Hodges, "Challenge to the New South: The Great Textile Strike in Elizabethton, Tennessee, 1929," *Tennessee Historical Quarterly* 23 (December 1964), 343–57; Bernstein, *Lean Years*, 1–43; U. S. Congress, Senate, *Working Conditions of the Textile Industry in North Carolina, South Carolina, and Tennessee*, Hearings on Sen. Res. 49, Senate Committee on Manufactures, 71st Congress, 1st Sess. (1929), 47–48. Bemberg and Glanzstoff were sibling companies. Though separate organizations, they shared the same leaders, and Dr. Adolf Mothwurf served as President of both.

2. "Labor — Southern Stirrings," *Time*, April 15, 1929, 13.

3. Tom Tippet, *When Southern Labor Stirs* (New York: Cape and Smith, 1931), 55.

4. The *Elizabethton Star* appeared Monday through Saturday. Its offices were right in the center of town, on the corner of Main Street and Elk Avenue. Frank H. Lovette was the *Star*'s editor and general manager; H. Richmond Campbell was managing editor.

5. "The Big Business Outlook," (editorial), *ES*, January 1, 1929, 3.

6. "Mr. Wolf is Visitor" (editorial), *ES*, January 9, 1929, 4.

7. Sherwood Anderson, "Elizabethton," *Nation*, May 1, 1929, 526.

8. "Greatness of South Looms as Inevitable," *ES*, January 10, 1929, 6.

9. "Local Plants Plan Monthly," and "Hoover Films to be Shown," *ES*, January 29, 1929, 1.

10. "Textile Plant Club Formed," *ES*, February 2, 1929, 1.

11. "Textile Employes Can Buy Homes" (editorial), *ES*, February 8, 1929, 4; also, "Textile Employes May Buy Homes By New Finance Plan," *ES*, February 7, 1929, 1; "Mothwurf Denies Houses Specified for New Employes," *ES*, February 5, 1929, 1.

12. "The Growth of Elizabethton" (editorial), *ES*, January 29, 1929, 4.

13. "Bringing in Outside Capital" (editorial), *ES*, February 6, 1929, 4.

14. "Why We Should Have 1000 Homes" (editorial), *ES*, February 14, 1929, 4.

15. Louis Stark, "The Meaning of the Textile Strike," *The New Republic*, May 8, 1929, 323–24.

16. "The Mighty South," (editorial), *CO*, May 15, 1929, 8.

17. "Piedmont Trade and Industry Flourish," *CO*, June 1, 1929, 1; "A Tale of Growth Beyond Equal: Romantic Story of North Carolina's Industrial Growth From the Smallest Beginnings," *CO*, June 2, 1929, IV, 1; "Will Tell of Piedmont Carolina's Lead in Textiles. Story Will Be Given Widest Distribution," *CO*, June 30, 1929, IV, 1.

18. Paul Gaston, *The New South Creed*; Ayers, *Promise.*

19. Charlotte was named after Britain's Queen Charlotte, hence the appellation "Queen City."

20. "Preparations for Camp for Confederate Veterans Here Will Be Started Monday," *CN*, April 14, 1929, 3; "Twenty-Six Units of National Guard of Two Carolinas to Parade in the City," *CN*, May 23, 1929, 5; "First of Visiting Confederate Veterans Reaches Charlotte for Reunion," *CN*, May 31, 1929, 30.

21. "The Confederates are Coming," (editorial), *MT*, May 9, 1929, 4; "The Reunion" (editorial), *MT*, June 6, 1929, 4; "Reunion was a Great Event" (editorial), *MT*, June 13, 1929, 4.

22. "Veterans of the Confederate Army Enjoy Reunion in Queen City," *MT*, June 6, 1929, 1. See also: "Confederate Flags In Breeze Bring Memories to Veterans," *CO*, May 26, 1929, II, 1; "Vanguard of Reunion Hosts Arriving," *CO*, June 2, 1929, 1; "City Hails Arrival of Veterans' Chief," *CO*, June 3, 1929, 1; "City Surrenders to Confederate Army," *CO*, June 4, 1929, 1; "'Dixie' Looses Full Fervor of Reunion," *CO*, June 5, 1929, 1; "Thousands Pour Into Charlotte for Vet's Reunion," *GDG*, June 3, 1929, 1; "Grey-Clad Warriors Make Merry in Annual Meet," *GDG*, June 4, 1929, 1.

23. "The Contradictory South" (editorial), *MT*, June 27, 1929, 4. For more reporting and commentary on the reunion see, for instance, "Reunion Advance To Arrive Today," *RNO*, June 2, 1929, 1; "Stars and Bars Floating Over Charlotte as Gray Hosts Meet," *RNO*,

Education section, June 2, 1929, 1; "Strong Early Rush of Civil War Vets to Annual Reunion," *GDN*, June 4, 1929, 1; "The Veterans' Reunion" (editorial), *GDN*, June 5, 1929, 6; "Festivities of Veterans Proceed at Lively Pace," *RNO*, June 6, 1929, 1.

24. "Confederate Flags in Breeze Bring Memories To Veterans," *CO*, May 26, 1929, II, 1.

25. Tom Tippett, a labor activist who rushed up to Elizabethton early in 1929, later described the financial situation of a male worker he knew. The man earned $12 per week, or $48 per month. Of his $48, he had to pay $25 for rent, $2.25 for light, and another $1.50 for water. That came to $28.75. That left $19.25 for food, clothing, and everything else, and that just wasn't near enough. The man worked twelve hours a day, six days a week, and the net result of all his labor was that every hour he worked he was driving himself and his family into debt. In fact, landlords and merchants and grocers in Elizabethton began to complain that the mill workers were constantly going deeper and deeper into debt; one grocer complained to Tippett that his mill worker customers all together owed him the extraordinary sum of $12,000. He agreed that the problem was not that the workers were deadbeats or profligates, but that no matter how hard they worked they somehow just ended up broke. Tippett, *Stirs*, 54. Also see: Letter from Charles Wood to Hugh Kerwin, March 16, 1929, Labor Conciliation Service, NA RG 280 170-4869. For Bowen's version of what happened, see Margaret Bowen, "The Story of the Elizabethton Strike," *American Federationist*, 36 (June 1912), 664-68; "Deadlock Seen In Mill Strike," *RNO*, March 15, 1929, 1.

26. "Sheriff Sees No Violence," *ES*, March 13, 1929, 1.

27. "The Glanzstoff Strike" (editorial) *ES*, March 15, 1929, 4.

28. "Strikers Hit Buck Little for Assault," *ES*, March 13, 1929, 1.

29. "Strikers Pick Committee to See Officials," *ES*, March 21, 1929, 1.

30. "Preliminary Report of Commissioner of Conciliation," RE: Glanzstoff, Elizabethton, Tenn., March 22, 1929; Letter from Charles Wood to Hugh Kerwin, March 22, 1929. Labor Conciliation Service, NA RG 280 170-4869; Telegram from Charles Wood to Hugh Kerwin, March 22, 1929, Labor Conciliation Service, NA RG 280 170-4869; "Strike Ends. Plants Open," *ES*, March 22, 1929, 1; "The Strike is Settled" (editorial), *ES*, March 22, 1929, 4; "Strike Ended At Two Rayon Plants," *RNO*, March 23, 1929, 2; Telegram from Alfred Hoffmann to Secretary of Labor James Davis, March 23, 1929. Labor Conciliation Service, NA RG 280 170-4869.

31. "Labor Leaders Missing," *ES*, April 4, 1929, 1; "Kidnaps Labor Men in Tennessee Strike," *NYT*, April 5, 1929, 10; "Labor Leaders Return - Governor to Act," *ES*, April 5, 1929, 1. For Hoffmann's account, see: "Armed Mob in South Kidnaps Organizer Hoffman," *The Hosiery Worker*, March 30, 1929, in Labor Conciliation Service, NA RG 280 170-4869.

32. "Labor Leaders Return - Governor to Act," *ES*, April 5, 1929, 1; "Labor Chiefs Back from 'Kidnapping' " *NYT*, April 6, 1929, 19.

33. "Green Promises to Prosecute Kidnappers," *ES*, April 8, 1929, 1.

34. "Excerpts: Telephone conversation 10:55 a.m. between Mr. H. L. Kerwin, Director of Conciliation, and Mr. Hoffman, of Elizabethton, Tennessee," April 16, 1929. Labor Conciliation Service, NA RRG 280 170-4869.

35. "Gen. Boyd is Arrested in Counter-Move," *ES*, May 17, 1929, 1; "Strikers Quieted in Tennessee Court," *NYT*, May 18, 1929, 40; "Hold Leaders of Textile Workers," *RNO*, May 19, 1929, 1.

36. "Quits as Mediator in Southern Strike," *ES*, May 11, 1929, 10; "Synopsis of Address

of Major George Berry," undated, Labor Conciliation Service, NA RG 280 170-4869.

37. "Mill Strike Ends at Elizabethton," *RNO*, May 26, 1929, 1; "Vote to End Big Strike at Elizabethton," *CO*, May 26, 1929, 1; "Rays of Sunshine in the Rayon War," *The Literary Digest*, June 8, 1929, Vol. CI, No. 10, 12.

38. The constitution of the company union is explained in: Federal Mediation Service, NA RG 280-170-4869, "Bemberg-Glanzstoff Council," January 1, 1930. The idea was to have a series of "plant councils" which would work to enhance the "mutual interest" of management and labor.

39. Undated flyer, Labor Conciliation Service, NA RG 280 170-4869.

40. Telegram from Anna Weinstock to Hugh Kerwin, June 10, 1929, Labor Conciliation Service, NA RG 280 170-4869; "Chronological Report of Strike at American Glanzstoff Company, Elizabethton," undated. Labor Conciliation Service, NA RG 280-170-4869; Letter from Anna Weinstock to Members of Local Union 1630, June 11, 1929, Labor Conciliation Service, NA RG 280 170-4869.

41. Telegram from Anna Weinstock to Hugh Kerwin, June 14, 1929, Labor Conciliation Service, NA RG 280 170-4869.

42. Letter from J. Clyde Donnelly and Margaret Bowen to Hugh Kerwin, September 18, 1929, NA RG 280 170-4869.

43. "Uses Tear Bombs to Rout Strikers," *NYT*, March 5, 1930, 6.

44. "Sheriff in Tennessee Quits Over Mill Strike," *NYT*, March 9, 1930, 1.

45. "Resolution Adopted at Citizens Meeting," Elizabethton, Tennessee, March 11, 1930, Labor Conciliation Service, NA RG 280-170-4869.

46. "Union Hall Attacked At Elizabethton, Tenn.," *NYT*, March 22, 1930, 3; "Urges Textile Inquiry, Citing 'New Outrage,'" *NYT*, March 23, 1930, II, 9.

47. Hodges, "Challenge," 357; Fred Beal and the NTWU, not surprisingly, denounced the deal as a sell-out, and NTWU activists in Elizabethton passed out handbills attaching the settlement; see: "'Communistic' Threat Mars Strikers Return," *CO*, May 28, 1929, 9. Jacquelyn Dowd Hall calls the settlement a "capitulation;" see her comments in "Disorderly Women," *Journal of American History*, Vol. 73, No. 2, September 1986, 368. In his history of the United Textile Workers, Robert R. R. Brooks summarizes the Elizabethton strike this way:

> the strike was called off when the union found no opportunity for settlement. Since the workers were going hungry, the end could not have been much longer avoided. The settlement, which was engineered by conciliators from the U.S. Labor Department, was hailed by the newspapers and the union as a victory. It was in reality a sweeping defeat. The union was not recognized and discharge or blacklisting of union members began as soon as the strike was over. All of the union's social and leadership functions were rapidly taken over by a company union set up by the company. The union maintained offices in the town for some time afterward but was nothing more than a focus of bitterness for the blacklisted workers. Robert R. R. Brooks, *UTW*, 314.

48. Virtually every issue of the *Charlotte Observer* published while the trial was in session, in the late summer and early fall of 1929, was filled with trial-related materials including extensive citations from trial testimony. Regarding the *Danville Register*, see, for instance, "Mills 3 and 4 to Close Down," *DR*, July 30, 1930, 1; "Gorman Attacks Policy of Mills," *DR*, July 31, 1930, 2; "Gorman Speaks At Mass Meeting," *DR*, August 24, 1939, 2.

49. "Explosion wrecks Stoney Creek Home," *ES*, May 10, 1929, 1; "No Clues Unearthed

in Investigation of Stoney Creek Blast," *ES*, May 11, 1929, 1; "Barn Near Valley Forge Burns Down at Midnight; Warning Note Found," *ES*, May 11, 1929, 1; "Bomb Found at Chair Plant," *ES*, May 13, 1929, 1; "150 Arrested on Picket Charge," *ES*, May 14, 1929, 1; "Martial Law not Likely," *ES*, May 15, 1929, 1; "Explosion Cuts Off City Water," *ES*, May 16, 1929, 1; "Court Hears Gap Creek Case," *ES*, May 23, 1929, 1.

50. Untitled editorial, *ES*, May 13, 1929, 1; "Editorial," *ES*, May 13, 1929, 1.

51. "Lawlessness Becomes Issue, Says Gardner," *CO*, September 17, 1929, 1.

52. "Registration Work Begun Today," *ES*, May 27, 1929, 1; "1500 Apply to Resume Work at Plants," *ES*, May 28, 1929, 1.

53. "Strike Near Conference Stage," *ES*, April 19, 1929, 1; "Conference Held to Plan Strike Action," *ES*, April 20, 1929, 1; "Strike Ends Second Week in Deadlock," *ES*, April 27, 1929, 1; "M'Grady Urges Settlement," *ES*, April 30, 1929, 1.

54. "Many Events Give Impetus to Optimism," *ES*, April 9, 1929, 1.

2

Hysteria and the Restoration of Order

The Elizabethton strike proved to be the prelude to a wave of spontaneous, leaderless, utterly unexpected, and to the southern press at least, shocking textile mill strikes. Everywhere throughout the southern Piedmont, millhands stormed out of their mills, paraded through their mill towns, and gave their betters a bad state of the jitters.

In South Carolina, for example, on April 1, 1929, some 300 textile workers walked off their jobs at the Woodruff Mills in Spartanburg. Two weeks later some 1200 workers walked out of the Brandon Mill in Greenville. The mood there was tense, and reporters complained of being "accosted" when they entered the mill village.[1] In Spartanburg some 900 workers walked out of another Brandon Corporation mill.[2] There, strike leaders vowed to remain nonviolent; they banned bootleggers from the strike scene and promised that strikers would stay within the law.[3] In Union another 1,000 workers walked off the job, complaining angrily about management's effort to squeeze out more productivity, something the workers derisively and angrily called "the stretch-out," and vowing not to return until the stretch-out ended.[4] Some 175 workers struck against the stretch-out in Anderson and there was a walkout in Newbury, too.[5]

Federal mediator Charles Wood rushed south from Elizabethton.[6] The South Carolina walkouts were spontaneous and unorganized, Wood reported back to Washington. The mood seemed "friendly" and the walkouts were "unmarked by violence of any kind."[7] None of the workers seemed interested in organizing a union; in Greenville workers at the Brandon Mill listened with irritation to a woman organizer from the United Textile Workers and then hustled her out of town.[8]

Millhands in the South Carolina towns often had widespread community support — after all, practically everybody in the little mill towns was kin to somebody in the mills — and the South Carolina strikes ended as quickly as they began, most often when management backed away from the extremes of the stretch-out.

Things were very different in North Carolina, however.

On April 1, 1929, workers in Gastonia walked out of the massive Loray Mill. It was not their first strike. In March 1928 superintendent Gordon Johnstone had implemented a stringent regime of cost-cutting and work intensification. Management saw this as simply a scientific means to boost productivity. Workers saw it as an outrageous attempt to extract more profit from their labor. In response, some fifty or more weavers and loom-fixers — skilled, self-confident, and highly paid workers — had walked off the job. But the strike was short-lived, the wages stayed cut, and the workers angrily went back.[9]

They went back out in April 1929, and their strike would be by far the best known of the 1929–31 strikes; it would attract national and international attention. Reporters from all over flocked to Gastonia. Gastonia, in the spring of 1929, was rocked by exuberant protests and tumultuous rallies. The North Carolina National Guard occupied the city, and combat troops patrolled outside the massive Loray Mill, the epicenter of the strike. Two people, Gastonia's police chief O. F. Aderholt and striker Ella May Wiggins, would be shot to death; scores would be injured and hundreds jailed. The turmoil culminated in the high ritual of the murder trial and conviction of the "Gastonia Seven," held in nearby Charlotte.[10]

The Gastonia strike, and the subsequent trial, became a grand cause for trade unionists, communists, civil libertarians, liberals, conservatives, southern traditionalists, progressives — just about everyone. Gastonia became, as Theodore Draper has remarked, symbolic of the entire strike wave.[11] Gastonia has, over the years, attracted considerable attention, including a fine study by John Salmond.[12]

Much of what occurred in Gastonia replicated what happened in Elizabethton. Angry millhands struck, protesting miserable wages, poor working conditions, and an authoritarian and distant management. Management responded with injunctions, scabs, the National Guard, and evictions. Many of the Loray millhands lived in company housing, and the company used evictions as a powerful weapon to repress strikers. In the end management won. It imprisoned the strikers, threw them out of their homes, and starved them out, reducing them to a ragtag, wornout, spent force. It was all drearily familiar.

Two things, however, and the poisonous interaction between them, made Gastonia different: the presence of Reds and the frantic reaction of the *Gastonia Daily Gazette*.

The *Gazette* was kin to the *Elizabethton Star* and most other southern hometown papers. It believed in progress and was sure that progress followed in the wake of capital. It nicely mixed nostalgia for the mythic Confederacy with optimism about the New South. Even as it spoke cheerily about progress, it staunchly defended the way things were and the powers that be. The only millhands in its pages were happy workers celebrating at jolly company-sponsored picnics.

If there was one amazing fact the reporting on the strikes revealed, it was this: the southern press was not at all monolithic; to the contrary, the southern press revealed an astonishing array of argument, analysis, and perspective. This is one of the prime lessons learned from studying the press's handling of the chaos in Gastonia.

The Gastonia strike was led by a score or so of yankee communists. They did not, to be sure, manufacture the discontent in the Loray mill. Mill management, the Manville-Jenckes Corporation, saw to that. The communists did, however, exploit and direct that discontent, and transform it into a raucous and outrageous carnival.

In 1928, in the wake of a bitter strike in New Bedford, Massachusetts, the American Communist Party decided to abandon its largely fruitless effort to take over the American labor movement. Instead, the communists tried to create their own parallel unions. Just after the New Bedford strike, the communists created the National Textile Workers Union as a rival to the United Textile Workers, an AFL union. The NTWU's lead organizer was a young man named Fred Beal. Beal came to Gastonia in January 1929 and had secretly begun recruiting members into the NTWU. When management, through its spies, heard about the organizing, they threatened to fire anyone talking union. When, on April 1, management carried out its threat, Beal openly called for a strike.[13]

Fred Beal's communist helpers were a flamboyant lot.[14] They were all yankees, mostly from New York or Boston, middle-class young people for the most part who had gone radical. Over the next few days, Gastonia was flooded by a troop of them. Though there were probably no more than a dozen or so in town at any one time, it seemed to some as if every imaginable Bolshevik in the world had swept into Gastonia. There was Vera Buch, now in her late thirties, a veteran labor militant; her future husband, Albert Weisbord, a Harvard-educated ideologue and, his many critics complained, an indefatigable self-promoter; Ellen Dawson, the fiery Scots radical; dashing George Pershing, one of the editors of The *Daily Worker*, movie-star handsome, who strolled along the picketline with a Kodak hanging from his neck; and youngsters like Sophie Melvin and Amy Schechter. The Reds, in turn, inspired a host of self-proclaimed super-patriots, anticommunists, and evangelists. The whole show attracted a horde of reporters from all over.

Gastonia was in for a turbulent three months. There were noisy parades and clashes with the police and National Guard almost every day. In mid-April, in the middle of the night, a gang of vigilantes wrecked the union's makeshift headquarters. Then, in early June, Gastonia's police chief, O. F. Aderholt, was shot to death during an altercation at union headquarters.

That was pretty much the end of the strike, but only the beginning of the strike story. All the union leaders were rounded up, and eventually seven, the "Gastonia Seven," were charged with murder. Their trial, in neighboring Charlotte, began in late August but quickly ended when one of the jurors had a nervous breakdown (there were no alternate jurors). When news of the mistrial swept through Gastonia, a mob of vigilantes attacked what was left of the strike headquarters, kidnapped and beat remaining union leaders, and even led a wild convoy of automobiles through Charlotte. Even that wasn't the end. In early September a crowd of vigilantes chased strikers out of Gastonia and opened fire on the strikers' truck. Ella May

Wiggins, who had become well known among union sympathizers for her union songs, was killed.

No wonder that Gastonia attracted such media attention.

Beal and the Gastonia Reds were precisely the sorts of people who would provoke outrage among many southerners. They were all outsiders and yankees, to boot; in an evangelically pious region, they were aggressive atheists; in a part of the country that had come to worship entrepreneurs, the communists were vehemently anticapitalist; in a society which prized highly ritualized behavior, the yankee communists were purposely obnoxious and provocative. The very things that the better classes in Gastonia so admired — church-going and profit-making, were openly mocked in their own streets. Worst of all, a great mob of millhands marched behind the outrageous communists.

Management reacted to the strike with a predictably hard line. Mill superintendent J. A. Baugh told the newspapers: "Our attitude, will be that we will not pay any attention to the strike whatsoever. . . . If necessary we will get workers immediately to replace those who have walked out. We are asking the strikers to vacate our houses. . . . The union is an I.W.W. bunch. . . . I think the situation will be over in a few days. Our home office, in Pawtucket, R. I., is not worried at all."[15]

All this was nervously recounted by the *Gastonia Daily Gazette*, Gastonia's only newspaper. The *Gazette* was clearly cousin to the *Elizabethton Star*. It was started in 1880 and ever since had been the voice of the textile industry. On its front page every issue of the *Gazette* announced: "Gaston County: The Combined Yarn Center of the South," and "Gastonia: The City of Spindles." The paper's reason for being was boosting the textile industry. In 1929 its editor, Hugh A. Query, was one of the city's respectable elite; in addition to running the paper, Query was an officer of the local American Legion.

On Wednesday, April 3, the third day of the strike, the *Gastonia Daily Gazette* published, under the banner headlines "Call Out Militia. Gastonia and Shelby Units are Ordered Out to Quell Loray Strike," a fearful account of the strike's early days. The *Gazette* reported an early clash between deputies and strikers: "From a happy, laughing, joking crowd, the demonstration became a belligerent, threatening mob, which threatened violence. Jeers, cat cries, and howls of derision greeted the deputies. . . . Fists were shaken and sticks and clubs waved in the air. . . . 'The situation is beyond our control' the mayor said to the governor."[16]

The images, of course, are straight out of an aristocrat's nightmare of revolutionary Paris; no wonder that, at least in the *Gazette*'s view, the mission of the National Guard was not simply to keep order, or, heaven forbid, protect strikers while exercising their constitutional rights, but rather, and bluntly, to "quell" the strike.

The same issue of the *Gazette* included an enormous full-page ad, paid for by unnamed "Citizens of Gaston County," which denounced Beal and the strikers in the most lurid terms. Beal, that "Red," and his coworkers, "who are apparently foreign," the ad shrieked, were "against all American tradition and American government . . . [and] against all religion. . . . The very existence, the happiness, and the very life even of every citizen of Gaston is threatened." The ad continued: "The question in the minds of many people who belong to the Christian church, who belong to the various patriotic and fraternal organizations is: Shall men and women of the type of Beal and associates, with their Bolshevik ideas, with their calls for violence and bloodshed, be permitted to remain in Gaston county?"[17]

Beal responded that he wasn't surprised by the *Gazette*'s ad because the paper was, afterall, nothing more than a tool of the bosses.

The *Gazette* responded angrily, in a front-page editorial, to Beal's claim. Its editors insisted that the *Gazette* was independent and nonpartisan, and that it was even sympathetic to the workers. The paper then fiercely denounced the "Russianized, Red, avowed Bolsheviks, who would destroy every capital, the very thing that makes it possible for any of us to work." The observation revealed two of the *Gazette*'s basic economic assumptions, shared, no doubt, by many of its readers. First, the interests of capital had economic and moral priority over the interests of labor; capital, afterall, is what "permits" workers to work. Second, though, since workers need the work capital permits them, it is obviously in the workers' own interest to advocate the cause of capital. In this sense, then, the interests of capital and labor are, by implication, identical.

The *Gazette* was not really interested in economic theory, though. It immediately returned to the rhetoric of apocalypse and terror: "Whenever the Communists get their bloody claws on America," the paper shouted, creating in the process a suitably sanguinary, bestial, and inhuman image of Beal and his comrades, "anarchy will reign and there will be no mills or factories to work in."[18]

The next day the *Gazette* ran an even more inflammatory full-page ad, again paid for by "Citizens of Gaston County." This one was called "Mob Rule vs. Law and Order." Again, the ad's discourse immediately escalated to apocalyptic invective:

> Every patriotic, law abiding American Citizen . . . yesterday . . . could see the difference between mob rule on the one hand and law and order on the other. Every American Citizen who loves his country and venerated its traditions could easily see the difference between the STARS AND STRIPES, the beautiful emblem of this Republic, and the blood red banner of Bolshevism, the flag of those who favor the destruction of all constitutional government, the flag of revolution and bloodshed, the flag of the country which does not believe in religion . . . [nor] the sanctity of marriage. . . . Before the troops arrived yesterday the mob was rampant at and near the Loray Mill in all of its seething hideousness, ready to kill, ready to destroy property. The troops arrived, men uniformed and armed, men true and loyal . . . and all became quiet and the mob dispersed. . . . THE STRIKE . . . WAS STARTED FOR THE PURPOSE OF OVERTHROWING THIS GOVERNMENT AND DESTROYING PROPERTY AND TO KILL, KILL, KILL![19]

Over the next few weeks, the *Gazette* would be the indefatigable hammer of the strikers. By May its anger abated somewhat, but the murder of Chief Aderholt reignited the *Gazette*'s fury. The paper's rhetoric was the rhetoric of panic, its language was filled with visions of blood-stained anarchy and prowling savage beasts, visions of eschatological nightmares in which nation, marriage, and religion are disemboweled by hideous, leering, aliens. It was the language of conspiracy and paranoia, of invasion and befoulment.[20]

There was a rhythm to the *Gazette*'s interpretation of events. After its initial explosion, the paper calmed down some. Then, not surprisingly, it flew into apoplexy again after the murder of Chief Aderholt. Even at its most furious, however, the *Gazette* combined its attacks on the Reds with calls for contributions to a "strikers' relief fund," which would help support ordinary millhands bankrupted or displaced by the bitter strike. Was this call a cynical move to defuse arguments that the *Gazette* was anti-worker? No doubt. But this was also an example of the contradictions in which the paper found itself. It was both a sturdy defender of capital and at least rhetorically the advocate of the common good. It wasn't always easy to jive the one with the other.[21]

To be fair to the *Gazette*, its sort of ferocious anticommunism was widespread. North Carolina's Senator Lee Overman, for instance, in defending his state's mill owners, insisted the strikes were concocted by outside agitators, "Communists" who sowed "the seeds of revolution, atheism, and free-lovism."[22] The *Southern Textile Bulletin*, the trade journal of the textile industry, was one of the most respected publications among mill managers. In the midst of the strike, its editor, David Clark, insisted that the "doctrine of free love, no religion, and social equality with negroes" were central communist beliefs. The Gastonia strike, Clark insisted, was provoked by assorted "radicals" and "communists," all connected to the Wobblies; "they profess to believe that Russia, with its socialism, social equality, free love, and atheism, is a heaven into which all workers should enter." The *Charlotte Observer* approvingly reported Clark's comments in a page-one story. And though the *Observer* was never quite as wild as the *Gazette*, it made it clear from the very beginning that it would have no truck with these "foreign, Russian, agitators."[23] The *Observer* carried front-page stories reporting that AFL trade-unionists, like the United Textile Workers president Ed McMahon, had denounced the communists; that federal mediator Charles Wood refused to speak with them; that the head of North Carolina's National Guard, General Metts, attacked them as "enemies of our government."[24]

Even moderate southerners were badly shaken by the Gastonia Reds. North Carolina's progressive governor, O. Max Gardner, for example, publicly defended everyone's right to free speech,[25] but privately fretted about communist subversion. In September 1929, after the Loray strike was long over, the Governor met with several textile executives and later reported to North Carolina Senators Overman and Simmons that "these gentlemen are convinced that the activity of the Communists in the Gastonia and Charlotte territory has vastly more significance than appears on the surface." He continued: "If the Communists have determined to make a stand in this state — and their literature indicates that they have — I am thoroughly of the opinion that drastic steps should be undertaken to rid this State of their presence."[26]

The epitome of this sort of interpretation of the Gastonia strike occurred at the end of the trial of the Gastonia Seven, in October 1929, when the prosecutor, John Carpenter, passionately demanded imprisonment of the accused.

At the end of the trial, in his final remarks to the jury, Carpenter began to recount the night of the shooting. He mimicked the mild questions of the Chief, and the cruel replies of the union guards; waving his arms, shrieking and hollering, he enacted the entire drama that occurred that night, himself starring in all the roles, now jumping into the air, now falling to the floor, now staring fiercely at the jurors. Judge Maurice V. Barnhill tried to gavel him to order, but Carpenter ignored the judge's warnings. He dropped to his knees and clutched the hand of Chief Aderholt's sobbing widow. He lurched to the prosecution table, snatched up the Chief's bloody shirt, waved it at the jurors yet again, and thrust it toward the widow, telling her softly, tears flooding his eyes, to "take it home."

None of the Yankee reporters had ever seen anything like it. "The tense crowd in the court room," wrote one reporter, "reacted to the solicitor's address with amazement." The *New York Times*, in an editorial, referred to it as a "stellar performance:"

> There have been histrionic efforts by lawyers before . . . but probably none ever rivaled in variety and gymnastics the exhibition given by this North Carolinian. Mr. Carpenter impersonated every actor in the drama, changing with protean skill from male to female. He sank to his knees, for the moment the wounded policeman returning the enemy's fire. He rolled on the floor, victim of the shot. He read from the Bible. He seized the hand of the widow . . . and pledged to her "the bleeding heart and tender sympathy" of the prosecution. He swore that he would be unworthy of his parents, his wife, and his children if he did not visit vengeance upon the defendants, he recited a catalogue of these estimable relatives. He wore out two boutonnieres, got dust and grease on his new blue suit, wilted his collar and made a rag of his tie. These were merely his physical demonstrations. In language the solicitor soared into the empyrean and beyond, knocking even at the gates of paradise and calling the attention of the Deity and the apostles to what the union agitators had done to Gastonia. Making tatters out of passions, he made shreds out of rhetoric and an oratorical combination salad out of figures of speech. Not the worst of these were the "cyclone and tornado which sank its fangs in the heart and life-blood of Gastonia."[27]

The *Gazette*'s ferocious opinions resonated widely. Yet they hardly reflected the unanimous opinion of the southern press.

Most southern newspapers, to be sure, were unequivocally hostile to the Gastonia communists. Many southern editors also thought that the *Gastonia Daily Gazette* had gone off its rocker, however. The *Greensboro Daily News*, for instance, commented acidly on the flaming full-page ad in the *Gastonia Daily Gazette* entitled "Mob Rule v. Law And Order!" The *Greensboro Daily News* noted that:

References to revolution, bloodshed, blood red banner, disbelief in marriage, religion, and God, the insistence on the purported determination "to kill, kill, kill," are, of course, the natural and inevitable phraseology which accompanies the mention of "communism" . . . but what puzzles the *Daily News* is what the sort of hysteria revealed in the advertisement is going to do to . . . Gastonia?[28]

Throughout the crisis the *Greensboro Daily News* again and again called for calm, nonviolence, and open and free negotiations between labor and capital. The *Daily News* placed the blame for the Gastonia vigilantes running amok in early September squarely on the "campaign of hate" launched, it said, by the *Gastonia Daily Gazette.*[29]

The *Raleigh News and Observer*, North Carolina's self-proclaimed progressive voice, consistently ridiculed what it considered to be the *Gazette*'s exaggerations. "Now is the time," the *News and Observer* mocked early on, "for all good patriots to look under their beds at night. The communists are coming." Of course, no one supports the Reds, said the *News and Observer*, but they are not the real problem.[30] The problem is that poor working conditions in the mills breed trouble. In fact, the *News and Observer* went on, the best way to prevent radicalism would be to encourage trade-unionism. By fighting so fiercely against responsible trade-unions, mill owners were only encouraging the radicals they so mightily feared. "If the radical labor element should ever get a foothold in the textile industry of the South," the *News and Observer* argued, "it will be because of the attitude of mill owners toward the efforts of the sane and conservative American Federation of labor and its textile group to organize the South."[31]

The *News and Observer*'s point revealed a curious way to read the problem of law and order. Southern journalists did indeed fret about chaos, but among them there was considerable disagreement about who threatened the social order most. To the *Gazette* and its allies, it was trade-unionists, strikers, outsiders, and Reds who threatened the South's status quo. But in the opinion of other papers, an even greater threat to social order came from the ultra right-wing vigilantes conjured up in part by the *Gazette*'s brand of hysteria.

Vigilante outrages repeatedly accompanied the strikes. In April vigilantes kidnapped union organizers Al Hoffmann and Ed McGrady in Elizabethton, and in Gastonia that month, they wrecked the union hall. In September, in the worst vigilante outburst, they kidnapped and beat union organizers, and murdered Ella May Wiggins. Throughout the entire period there was, as reporter Mary Vorse warned her friend Vera Buch, one of the Gastonia strike leaders, something "lynchy" in the air. "I've been in so many of these situations," Vorse told Buch, "I can smell it."[32] Crosses were burned on hills around Elizabethton. In every strike town there were unexplained explosions and midnight shootings. Ironically, it was the self-styled defenders of law and order who, even more than the unionists or even the communists, had become the greatest threats to law and order.

The southern press was almost as hostile to the right-wing vigilantes as it was to the communists. In April, just after vigilantes had wrecked the union headquarters in Gastonia, the *Charlotte Observer* published a long letter to the editor that well expressed the position the *Observer* itself would take. The letter was written by a W. E. Simpson who identified himself as a mill worker. Simpson wrote:

The action of the masked mob in destroying the headquarters of the National Textile Workers Union was a black spot on the name of Gastonia and Gaston County. I am not a union man . . . but I want to say here that this act made more friends for Beal at the mill . . . than anything that has been done. And whatever may be said or done about the actions of the mob, all cotton mill workers will forever believe that the workers were sent out at the Loray mill at 2 o'clock in the morning with the fire axes and crowbars . . . with orders to wreck the building. . . . And I want to say this to the newspapers, that the mill workers believe the papers are being controlled by the mill owners and that they only publish stuff as suits the mill owners. In the mill worker of 10 years ago and the mill worker of today you have a different person. They are not so easy to believe anything that the man uptown says, as they were then. They have learned to think for themselves. . . . I have worked in the mills of Gaston County for 20 years and I see more unrest, more determination to take things in their own hands and find a remedy for their condition than ever before. Long working hours, low pay, curtailment and being forever driven like a dumb brute is causing a feeling of revolt . . . the mill workers have made up their minds that in unions is their only life, and they are going to organize. . . . We are going to have unions.[33]

That the notoriously anti-union *Observer* elected to publish such a letter, at the very same time that it was so angrily attacking the Gastonia communists, demonstrates, at the very least, that the *Observer*'s own position on the strikes was not without contradiction.

Most papers in the southern Piedmont were appalled by the mob violence directed against union organizers. Week after week, for instance, the *Raleigh News and Observer* denounced vigilantism, and noted that scores of other state newspapers shared its opinion — for instance, the *Greensboro Daily News*, the *Fayetteville Advocate*, the *Warren Record*, the *Chapel Hill Weekly*, the *Hickory Record*, and the *Shelby Star*. All these papers agreed that anti-union vigilantism was a disgrace to the old North state.[34] The *Richmond Times-Dispatch* described vigilantism, regardless of its target, as a reflection of "not a desire to promote the ends of justice, but a base and cowardly desire to inflict pain and torture upon a defenseless person." The *Times-Dispatch* continued: "In every instance, the members of such mobs should be treated as outlaws and jailed without consideration for the their standing in the community."[35]

The killing of Chief Aderholt in June 1929, and then Ella May Wiggins in September, shocked everyone. When, for example, the University of North Carolina's Frank Porter Graham heard of Wiggin's killing, he wrote fellow reformer, journalist Nell Battle Lewis: "I have never felt more depressed and bewildered in my life than I did in reading Sunday's paper with the story of Mrs. Wiggins' death. Her death is upon the heads of us all. . . . While the killing depressed me there was also something lifting about it to me. Her faith and her courage are a vindication of the spirit and ideals of our North Carolina.[36]

With Graham's permission Lewis published portions of his note in the papers. Not everyone agreed with Graham and Lewis. When David Clark, of the *Southern Textile Bulletin*, read Graham's remarks some months later, he was furious. In response, Clark wrote:

Ella May Wiggins was not a widow but a woman whose husband had left her. Her reputation was so bad that she had, long before she ever heard of communism, been requested to move out of several mill villages. She was a "hard-boiled" type of woman who loved a quarrel and a fight. . . . Frank Graham's effort to create a martyr is ludicrous. . . . The most regrettable part of the letter . . . is his effort to justify and defend the communists who murdered Chief Aderholt.[37]

Still, the southern press overwhelmingly was appalled by the anti-union violence. In editorial after editorial the *Raleigh News and Observer* fretted about the situation in North Carolina. Shocked by the violence tearing at the state, the *N & O* insisted that something was very wrong with the state's arrangement of wealth and power that would have to be righted before there could be peace.[38]

The *News and Observer*'s painful editorial of September 12, 1929, entitled "Two Views of Mob Violence,"[39] is particularly interesting because it includes not only an analysis of the situation, but a debate with other North Carolina newspapers.

The editorial begins by mourning that the good impression created by Judge M. V. Barnhill's handling of the Charlotte trial of the Gastonia Seven had now been ruined by vigilante outbreaks in Gaston and Cabarrus Counties: "The mob that organized in Gastonia without restraint, that made a demonstration in Charlotte without apprehension, and committed a heinous crime in Cabarrus without detection, did much to undo the good opinion which Judge Barnhill's court insured for North Carolina justice."

Next, the *News and Observer* makes a crucial point. It accepts that fighting communism is good. It insists, however, the "introduction of Anarchy as the foe of communism would weaken those who oppose either or both."

Curious here is a shift in the usual use of "mob" and "Anarchy." In southern papers both terms were dangerous and frightening words. Most often they were applied to strikers, trade-unionists, and communists. Here, oddly, they are now applied to the hyper-patriotic, ultra-conservative vigilantes.

The *News and Observer* next, and surprisingly, praises the *Gastonia Gazette*, which the *News and Observer* had mocked so often. "The *Gastonia Gazette*," the *N & O* argued, "takes the right view . . . [when] it says that . . . 'We have, perhaps, been more sinned against than sinning in Gastonia,' but that should not give unbridled license to mob members, no matter how keenly they feel about this thing."

On the other hand the *N & O* angrily went after the *Charlotte News*, normally a fellow "progressive" paper. The *News*, responding to the vigilante outbreaks, had published an editorial called "Nerves Do Snap," which, while condemning the vigilantes, nevertheless insisted that, in the vigilantes' defense, one should recall the terrible outrages and provocations of the communists. The *N & O* was appalled by the *News*'s editorial. The editorial was "regrettable;" it only justified the absurd notion of fighting Communism with Anarchism.

The *N &O* then concluded with what it considered to be a critical distinction between cause and effect. The Gastonia communists were not the cause of the troubles in Gastonia; they were an effect. The real cause was the decision by the "Pawtucket, R. I." owners of the Loray mill to cut wages and intensify labor via the "stretch-out." The cause of Gastonia's troubles was corporate oppression, not communist agitation; the effect was worker outrage and the arrival of communists looking for trouble. Had management reduced the work week to fifty-five hours, as a number of mills already had done; had management abandoned the "stretch-out" and paid decent wages and had management recognized the right of workers to join or not to join a union, "there would not be a trace of communism among the workers of any Gastonia mill."

"Two Views of Mob Violence" is a remarkable editorial. Written quickly to meet the day's deadline, it clearly demonstrates the diversity of opinion within the southern press. In many ways quite traditional — the hostility to communism, the irritation with Yankee outsiders (the designation of the Loray Mill's owners not by their corporate name, Manville-Jenkes, but by their regional location, "Pawtucket, R. I.," was surely not accidental), the pervasive fear of disorder — "Two Views" expresses the continuing strength of familiar discourse. But it shows too that more than a few southern papers were actually sympathetic not only to workers but to trade-unions. It shows that the *N & O*, at least, saw itself, and the press in general, as not simply an agent of the market (and particularly the textile industry), but as a voice independent of the market, a voice concerned with the market, too, but with a much wider if still evolving concept of the commonweal.

NOTES

1. "Greenville Strikers Reject Offer," *CO*, April 4, 1929, 12. The strike was resolved after about a week, when management agreed to drop the stretch-out; see "Accord Gains At Greenville," *CO*, April 9, 1929, 2.

2. "Brandon Mill Still Tied Up," *CO*, April 4, 1929, 12.

3. "Strikers Put Ban on Violence," *CO*, April 5, 1929, 3.

4. "Union Strikers Firm in Stand," *CO*, April 4, 1929, 12; "No Change in Strike Situation at Union," *CO*, April 9, 1929, 2.

5. "Workers Strike at Anderson," *CO*, April 5, 1929, 3; "Probers Blame Mill Officials for Walk-Out," *CO*, April 5, 1929, 1.

6. "U.S. Labor Commissioner Seeking to End Strike," *CO*, Tuesday, April 2, 1929, 3. The Brandon and Poinsett Mills were struck in Greenville; the Buffalo Mill was struck in Union.

7. "The South Carolina Strikes," editorial, *CO*, Tuesday, April 2, 1929, 8.

8. "Strikers Look to Conference," *CO*, Wednesday, April 3, 1929, 2; "Greenville Strikers Resent Presence of Foreign Agitator," *CO*, Wednesday, April 3, 1929, 2.

9. "Weavers of Loray on Strike; Cut in Wages Their Reason," *GDG*, March 5, 1928, 5; "Striking Weavers of Loray Still Out," *GDG*, March 6, 1928, 1.

10. Vorse's *Strike!* is a fictional recounting of the Gastonia strike. Anderson's *Beyond Desire* echoes in part the Gastonia events, and William Rollins, author of *The Shadow Before Me* was a reporter in Gastonia. The other fictions include at least some reference to Gastonia. Fred Beal's memoirs, *Proletarian Journey* include, of course, a long discussion of what happened in Gastonia, as do Vera Buch's memoirs. Liston Pope's *Millhands and Preachers* (New Haven: Yale University Press, 1942) was the first detailed study of the strike; Pope focuses on the role of churches and preachers in Gastonia's society. Pope's pathbreaking study inspired the later *Spindles and Spires* (Atlanta: John Knox, 1976), by John R. Earle, Dean D. Knudsen, and Donald W. Shriver, which continues an examination of the issues Pope raised. Theodore Draper's "Gastonia Revisited," *Social Research* Vol. 38 (Spring 1971), No. 1, 3–29, provides both a solid summary of the strike events and a concise discussion of the communists' role in the those events. Williams' *The Thirteenth Juror*, in a polemical narrative by local authors who blame events primarily on the communist agitators who invaded Gastonia. Salmond's *Gastonia: 1929* (Chapel Hill: University of North Carolina, 1996) is the definitive narrative.

11. Draper, "Gastonia Revisited," 28.

12. Salmond, *Gastonia.*

13. "Strikers in Gaston Backed by Communist," *CO*, April 2, 1929, 1; "Half of Loray Mill Employes Out in Strike," *CN*, April 2, 1929, 1; "Agitator Busy with Workers," *CO*, Tuesday, April 2, 1929, 3; "Order Out Troops in Gastonia Mill Strike," *CN*, April 3, 1929; 1; "Quiet Prevails in Loray Strike Situation," *CN*, April 4, 1929, 1; "Troops Sent to Gastonia," *RNO*, April 4, 1929; 1; "Clashing Forces Mark Time in Gastonia Strike," *RNO*, April 5, 1929, 1; "Sees Danger in Red Propaganda," *RNO*, April 6, 1929, 1.

14. Beal and his associates made no effort to conceal their political sympathies. At the very beginning of the strike, Beal told reporters:

> This is the first strike of our national union . . . and we intend to make it a big success. . . . We feel confident that this Loray strike will be the beginning of a tremendous south-wide movement to organize thoroughly in every state. We are receiving aid in our strike from George Pershing, representing the *Daily Worker*, the official organ of the Communist Party of America. Our union, however, is not connected with the Communist Party, but after our union is granted its demands, the Communist group will come in with its political-educational program. . . . The union was organized here about six months ago. . . . We decided to come out in the open and not to hide but to tell the world that we belonged to the union and believe in it. We believe in this country that we have a right to organize a union and we will fight for that right.

See "Strikers in Gaston Backed by Communist," *CO*, April 3, 1929, 1; "Loray Mill Runs At Half Capacity," *RNO*, April 3, 1929, 1.

15. "Strikers . . .", *CO*, April 4, 1929, 1.

16. "Call Out Militia," *GDG*, April 3, 1929, 1.

17. "History of the Loray Strike," *GDG*, April 3, 1929, 7.

18. "The Workers' Friend" (editorial), *GDG*, April 4, 1929, 1.

19. "Mob Rule vs. Law and Order," *GDG*, April 4, 1929, 7.

20. Virtually all of the *Gazette*'s front-page editorials in April continue to mix interest and frantic accusation. The *Gazette* insisted on its own independence, and even admitted the right of labor to organize; but then it hammered on the "Red Russians" in our midst who would "destroy all Property!" See, for instance, "Time for Sober Thought" (editorial), *GDG*, April 5, 1929, 1. Proclamations paid for by the unnamed "Citizens of Gaston County" were far more hysterical than the *Gazette*'s own editorials. An April 5 ad warned: "Red Russianism Lifts Its Gory Hands Right Here in Gastonia;" "Red Russianism . . . ," *GDG*, April 5. 1929, 12. A later ad announced a mass rally to hear inspirational speaker Joe Mitchell explain the differences between "Americanism" and "Communism;" "Mass Meeting . . . ," *GDG*, April 24, 1929, 5. Regarding Chief Aderholt's murder, see, for instance, "A Deep Laid Scheme" (editorial), *GDG*, June 8, 1929, 4, which explains that the murder of Chief Aderholt, and the whole strike for that matter, was a "deep-laid plot."

21. "Strikers' Relief Fund," *GDG*, May 3, 1929, 1.

22. "Farmers Dominate Gastonia Trial Jury," *NYT*, October 4, 1929, 19.

23. David Clark, "Communism," *STB*, September 19, 1929, 17. See: "Clark Scouts Importance of Youth's Strike at Gastonia: Publisher declares Communistic Program of Free Love and Inter-Racial Intercourse Misses Fire," *CO*, April 6, 1929, 1. For a sample of the *Observer*'s opinion, see: "IWW-ism Arrives" (editorial), *CO*, April 4, 1929, 8; "An Impossible Strike" (editorial), *CO*, April 5, 1929, 8; "Communists Threaten Sweeping Textile Strike," *CO*, April 6, 1929, 1; "The Difference" (editorial), *CO*, April 7, 1929, 8.

24. The papers were full of reports of attacks on the Gastonia Reds. See, for instance: "Loray Strike Condemned by U.S. Agent," *CO*, April 6, 1929, 1; "Strike Chief Alarm Metts," *CO*, April 6, 1929, 1; "M'Mahon Flays Red Union As Exploiting Americans," *CO*, April 12, 1929, 1.

25. When he heard of the vigilante raid on union headquarters in Gastonia, on April 18, 1929, Gardner told his cabinet: "I immediately gave out the statement in which I stated that the policy of North Carolina does not countenance violence on the part of any person . . . [and] that in North Carolina a man may join whatever he wants to join, even the Communistic Party, and not forfeit his right to protection of property and person." Report to the Council of State, May 9, 1929, Governor Gardner Papers, File 112, N.C. State Archives.

26. Letter from Governor O. Max Gardner to Senators Overman and Simmons, September 23, 1929, Gardner Papers, File 112, N. C. State Archives; Letter from Treasury Secretary H. Mellon, to Senator F. M. Simmons, September 26, 1929, Gardner Papers, file 112, N. C. State Archives; Letter from Senator Lee S. Overman to Governor O. Max Gardner, October 5, 1929; Letter from Governor O. Max Gardner to Senator Lee S. Overman, October 8, 1929, Gardner Papers, File 112, N. C. State Archives.

27. "Varied Types of Oratory Employed in Murder Case," *RNO*, October 18, 1929, 1; "Judge to Charge Aderholt Jury," *CO*, October 19, 1929, 1; "Where Oratory Still Witches" (editorial), *NYT*, October 21, 1929, 26.

28. "Two Exhibits" (editorial), *GDN*, April 6, 1929, 6.

29. See, for instance, "The State and the Mob" (editorial), *GDN*, April 20, 1929, 6; "Sitting Quietly and Calmly" (editorial), *GDN*, April 21, 1929, 6; "It Demands Action," *GDN*, April 23, 1929, 6; "The Natural Result of Campaigns of Hate" (editorial), *GDN*, September 11, 1929, 6.

30. "The Communist Bugaboo," *RNO*, April 6, 1929, 4.

31. "Fuel to the Fire" (editorial), *RNO*, April 5, 1929, 4; see also: "Somebody Call a Cop!" (editorial), *RNO*, April 7, 1929, 4.

32. Vera Buch, *A Radical Life*, 219.

33. "The Contentions of a Mill Worker," letter from W. E. Simpson, *CO*, April 23, 1929, 8.

34. See, for instance, "And We Learn About Reds from Them" (editorial), *RNO*, April 19, 1929, 4; "North Carolina Looks to the Governor" (editorial), *RNO*, April 21, 1929, 4; "The State and the Mob," from the *Greensboro Daily News*, *RNO*, April 22, 1929, 4; "Action and Quick Action" (editorial), *RNO*, April 23, 1929, 4; "Gastonia's High Duty" (editorial), *RNO*, April 25, 1929, 4; "Justice and Only Justice" (editorial), *RNO*, April 26, 1929, 4; "The Record Thus Far," from the *Greensboro News*, *RNO*, April 26, 1929, 4; "The Gastonia Outrage," from the *Fayetteville Advocate*, *RNO*, April 27, 1929, 4; "A Challenge," from the *Warren Record*, *RNO*, April 27, 1929, 4; "A Disgrace" from the *Chapel Hill Weekly*, *RNO*, April 28, 1929, 4; "Mob Against Mob," from the *Hickory Record*, *RNO*, April 29, 1929, 4; "Should Run Them Down," from the *Shelby Star*, *RNO*, April 29, 1929, 4.

35. "Mob Violence" (editorial), *RT-D*, August 23, 1930, 4.

36. Letter to Nell Battle Lewis from Frank Porter Graham, September 23, 1929, SHC, UNC-CH, Graham Papers, 1819-Series 1-1929-1.

37. Editorial from the *Southern Textile Bulletin*, April 10, 1930, 22, in Graham Papers, SHC, UNC-CH, 1819-Series 1-1930-24.

38. See, for instance: "The Why of the Troops" (editorial), *RNO*, September 9, 1929, 4; "Two Views of Mob Violence" (editorial), *RNO*, September 12, 1929, 4; "The Press on Mobs and Communists" (editorial), *RNO*, September 14, 1929, 4; "Gastonia in Death's Shadow" (editorial), *RNO*, September 16, 1929, 4; "The Thirteenth Juror" (editorial), *RNO*, September 17, 1929; "The Antidote to Communism" (editorial), *RNO*, September 18, 1929, 4; "Fighting Fire with Fire" (editorial), *RNO*, September 19, 1929, 4; "The Truth of the Gastonia Situation and the Remedy" (editorial), *RNO*, September 22, 1929, 4.

39. "Two Views of Mob Violence" (editorial), *RNO*, September 12, 1929, 4.

3

Metaphors of Struggle

Reporting from Gastonia the day after the strike began, the *Charlotte Observer*'s reporter on-the-scene wrote that everyone in town was edgy and nervous, that everyone was filled with "dread"; the strike, the reporter concluded, was "a drama . . . that may have a dozen denouements."[1] A front-page report of the same event in the *Charlotte News* spoke of "a mysterious silence" settling over the beleaguered town.[2] The vagueness of the reports demonstrated as much as anything else the southern press's utter unfamiliarity with the story that was breaking. Though most reporters were native Southerners, few if any knew anything about labor and trade-unions, and as for the millhands, they were an utterly alien caste. That the reporter thought of the strike as a "drama," though, is important. The strike, somehow, was like a drama; it had a setting, a beginning, and presumably an end. It had an often remarkable cast of characters and above all, it had conflict.

More than almost anything else, it was the conflict of the strikes that attracted reporters' attention. Strikes are, by nature, violent events. Two rights collide in a strike — the right of employers to hire and fire and control their own property, and the right of employees to withdraw their labor and use their rights to freedom of speech and freedom of assembly to advance their cause. Sooner or later industrial societies develop elaborate codes of labor law to regulate and defuse this collision, but the South in 1929 was still a young industrial society and there were few rules governing the fight between mill owners and millhands.

The textile strikes were cloaked in violence. In all the strike centers, mysterious explosions ruptured the nights, and masked men fired at their opponents' homes. Every day there were clashes on the picket-lines between strikers and scabs, strikers and police.

In this battle both sides engaged in violence, but the balance of forces was overwhelmingly in management's favor. It was hardly a fair fight, and in the end management shattered every strike and drove the exhausted workers either out of town or back into the mills.

The violence of the strikes created that odd and ominous mood reporter Mary Vorse thought she could smell;[3] it was what the *Charlotte Observer* reporter had in mind when describing the mood in Gastonia the night the National Guard deployed in town. That night the reporter wrote in the *Observer*'s headline story, "a nervous quietude . . . prevailed . . . after a hectic day crowned with the mobilization of five National Guard companies to quell menacing disturbances and remove the threat of mob violence."[4]

Strikes meant transgression; they meant violations; they meant law-breaking. It was little wonder then that newspapers like the *Elizabethton Star* and the *Gastonia Daily Gazette*, for example, consistently associated strikes, trade-unions, and union organizers, with chaos and crime. It was little wonder that the press's recurring theme was the need to restore law and order. Threats to the social order, the "menacing disturbances" and the threat of "mob violence" that concerned the *Observer*'s reporters, were, of course, associated almost exclusively with workers. They were the menacing ones; they were the perpetrators of "mob violence." The better classes, the forces of order, the police, the deputy sheriffs, and the National Guard had no choice but to contain and repress this "mob."

Stories often conveyed a vague but palpable sense of the "grand peur" evoked by the strikers. On April 6, 1929, for instance, the *Charlotte Observer* reporter in Gastonia described an entirely peaceful rally, but ended the story noting that "trouble seemed brewing" and the people were "restless." The story ran below a headline warning that the "Communists Threaten" more strikes. That bold headline, "Communists Threaten," in innumerable versions, would stalk many southern newspapers for more than a year.[5] Indeed, "threat," and synonyms like "menace," were favorite nouns and verbs among reporters, as in *Charlotte News* stories that spoke of "strike threats," and workers "threatening" the Loray Mill."[6]

There were many variations on this theme. It is important to note that on occasion, roles were reversed in the press, and at least briefly, the forces of order assumed the notorious role of the mob.

When the textile strike began in Danville, Virginia, in the fall of 1930, some community leaders were eager for Virginia's Governor John Pollard to send in the National Guard. The *Richmond Times-Dispatch* warned against the idea, however. The situation was not out of hand and there was no reason to believe that it would get out of hand. The problem was, the *Times-Dispatch* argued, that "the presence of military forces on an occasion like this tends to incite disorder rather than stave it off. Americans regard uniformed men on duty at a strike which is being conducted along peaceful lines as a show of tyranny. . . . Many strikes have been turned into riots by reason of blundering in this respect on the part of civil officials."[7]

Troops were sent in anyway. The *Richmond Time-Dispatch* thought it a terrible business. It insisted that use of combat troops to keep order in an industrial dispute was bad policy indeed. As for the Pittsylvania county authorities who pleaded with the Governor for the troops, the *Times-Dispatch* mocked that they "have whined before they have been hit." It wrote, "Because of a lack of knowledge of their own responsibilities or a lack of courage, they have subjected their own community to the indignity of having State troops ordered in to make the people behave themselves."[8]

Just a few weeks later, a National Guard patrol opened fire one night on a car that failed to halt at their command. Though badly wounded, the driver survived. It turned out he was a bootlegger, running some sixty gallons of white lightning into Danville. The *Danville Register* was not particularly sympathetic to him, but was worried nevertheless. "Are the military patrols to fire on every car that refuses to halt at command?" the paper asked. Danville, and its working-class suburb, Schoolfield, were not under martial law, the paper pointed out. However necessary the state military might be, the paper argued, it is essential that local civilian authorities retain control of the situation and not surrender to the military. The threat to Danville's republican freedoms, the paper implied, came not so much from labor radicals as from the ostensible forces of order.[9]

An even more dramatic incident of this sort had occurred earlier in Gastonia, in April 1929. On April 22 the Gastonia strikers staged a grand march protesting the vigilantes' destruction of their headquarters. The National Guard had only recently been withdrawn, and Gastonia's hard-pressed authorities had hastily deputized a large number of men recruited not from Gastonia's population at large but from among men known to be hostile to unions — plant policemen, for instance, and American Legion militants. Strikers bitterly complained that these "special deputies" all too often were little more than thugs.

On April 22 the Gastonia strikers marched in their parade. Accompanying them was Legette Blythe, the *Charlotte Observer*'s star reporter. As the crowd approached the Loray mill, a mass of special deputies, armed with blackjacks, night sticks, and shot guns, rushed the head of the column. The parade collapsed in chaos as the people up front frantically scrambled to the rear to escape the assault. One deputy cracked his blackjack against the head of a man he assumed to be a striker; the man was, in fact, reporter Blythe.

Despite his injuries, Blythe filed his despatch with the *Observer*. "I was in Gastonia and on the scene of battle," he began, "when the striking textile workers . . . marching in a body with the avowed purpose of forming a picket line at the mill were met this afternoon by a force of Gastonia police and special deputies." The head of the column reached the mill and was confronted by police led by Chief Aderholt. "Did they have a parade permit?" Aderholt asked. The strikers replied that they hadn't.

It was then, Blythe continued, that the chaos began. The more experienced police officers began arresting strikers. There was pushing and shoving, and suddenly, groups of special deputies began wading in with nightsticks and blackjacks. Blythe wrote, "Strikers who appeared in any way belligerent or who 'talked back' were immediately arrested and many of them were bodily thrown into waiting automobiles. . . . It appeared to be a desperate situation. . . . A number of the special deputies . . . in their apparent unnerved condition were guilty of much brutality that was neither necessary nor excusable."

"I saw old men and old women knocked off or pushed off the street simply because they couldn't get along fast enough," Blythe continued.

> One old woman was dragged from in front of the relief store and with one officer twisting her arm and others pulling her was thrown into a waiting car. . . . "They are running us out of our store and our babies hain't got nothin' to eat at home. How come they are doing us like that?" I heard one old woman crying out in her distress. "I don't see how come us poor folks don't get no chance. If they was not a-goin' to let us strike, how come they let these fellows come down here from the north in the first place and get us all messed up like this?"

Blythe praised the majority of officers who did their duty. Some of the special deputies, he insisted, however, "acted in a manner of the brutal reprobates that they must be and it was their actions that have brought a certain amount of stigma upon the city and its conscientious police officers."[10]

The April 22 battle was a disaster. Mercifully, no one was killed but dozens were injured. At least twenty-four strikers were arrested. Federal mediator Charles Wood laconically summarized the riot in a telegram to his superiors in Washington: "Militia removed from Gastonia today. Reds staged parade in violation ordinance. Got in conflict with police. Small local riot. Local newspaper reporter slugged by guard. Bad situation made worse by poor handling."[11]

In its editorial on the riot, entitled "Lawlessness by Law Enforcers," the *Charlotte News* argued that "it is evident that those who have been left to represent the law in Gaston County in view of the withdrawal of State troops ought to be taken off to school somewhere before being put on duty and instructed in what this thing of law is all about. They don't seem to understand it exactly."

The behavior of the special deputies, the *News* concluded, was "ludicrous," "disquieting," and "disheartening."[12]

Mayor W. T. Rankin and Solicitor John Carpenter condemned the attack on the strikers and apologized for the assault on the reporter. Newspaper reports, so often hostile to the strikers, now condemned the authorities and especially the special deputies. The *Observer* noted that "there has been considerable criticism of the character of some of the deputies employed."[13] The killing of six strikers by deputies in Marion, in early October 1929, renewed the concern that at least in some cases, the "mob" might in fact be found on the respectable side of the battle.[14]

If images of violence and transgression dominated news reports, they were hardly the only metaphors deployed. Images of fire and storm, for example, were frequent. In September 1930, on the eve of the strike there, the *Danville Register* reported a fight in front of union headquarters with the ominous headline: "First Violence in Organization of Textile Workers Breaks Calm: Strike Now Believed To Be Imminent," the "calm" presumably being the proverbial calm-before-the-storm.[15] *Time*'s southern correspondent compared the strikes to "fire in broom straw," and some variation on this theme was typical. Reporting on strikes in Spartanburg,

South Carolina, for instance, the *Charlotte Observer* told its readers that "the flame of unrest flared anew." Mixing metaphors, the same report noted that "the storm . . . has been brewing since last Friday."[16]

The message of these sorts of metaphors was that the strikes, like wildfires and storms, were ultimately unpredictable and irrational natural events. One could, perhaps, put out fires, but the most one could do with storms was to ride them out. Such metaphors were ultimately unsatisfactory, among other reasons, because they translate drama into meteorology. Perhaps this helps explain why the most insistent metaphors were not drawn from fire departments and weather reports but from the world of war.

Again and again, reporters used military metaphors to describe the events that had engulfed the region — "Textile Mill Officials, 4000 Strikers, Set For Long Siege In South Carolina," ran a typical headline, this one in the *Charlotte News*.[17] The turmoil, these metaphors argued, was not exactly a species of criminal behavior, nor was it simply an act of God, like a forest fire or a hurricane. Rather, these military metaphors argued, the turmoil was a clash between human beings, arrayed in two opposing armies, each struggling to achieve a victory.

Certainly the vivid memories of World War I had something to do with all this, as did the immediate militarization of the strikes that occurred when the National Guard was rushed in. Perhaps an older obsession with invasion and traumatic war produced some of the stock of military metaphors the reporters used. Whatever their origin, reporters consistently described the strikes as, fundamentally, a war.

Elizabethton, the *Charlotte Observer* reported, looked like a "combat zone" in early May 1929, when the Bemberg-Glanzstoff management attempted to reopen the mills under the protection of the National Guard. "In a warlike setting," the *Observer* reported, "with a cordon of machine guns in position and national guardsmen in trench helmets drawn up in company formation, the gates of the Bemberg mills . . . will open tomorrow." With, by the reporter's count, nearly 6,000 angry workers massed on the picket line, however, the situation was "tense."[18]

The next day, the *Observer* reported, the Elizabethton plants had reopened "under the ominous nozzles of machine guns mounted on roofs." A "war of words and warrants" had engulfed Elizabethton, the *Observer* concluded.[19] By mid-May things in Elizabethton were spinning out of control; as a *New York Times* reporter noted, "affairs were drifting to open warfare."[20] Reporting on Gastonia early in that strike, the *Charlotte News* entitled a front-page story "Quiet Prevails in Loray Strike Situation — Over Two Hundred Guardsmen Keep Grim Watch As Strikers Threaten Loray Mill — Sudden Orders Lend War-Like Air to Grounds."[21]

Military metaphors were ubiquitous. The *New York Times* reporter in Marion spoke of "an atmosphere of veritable civil war." The *Greensboro Patriot* warned of "the bloodiest and bitterest commercial war on record;" and *The New Republic* insisted that the war in the South was a class war, the thing "that the Communists call by that name — raw."[22]

For southern papers in particular, a crucial subset of this military imagery was the theme of invasion. Echoing by now almost primeval fears of abolitionist subversives and yankee predators, papers insisted that the strikes erupted because of an invasion by "foreign agitators." "No greater affliction could be wished upon the textile operators in the South," the *Charlotte Observer* argued, "than that they should come under the dominating influences of these foreign agitators. . . . It would mean a farewell to the contented life the Southern operatives have been living."[23]

To be sure, the press did make distinctions. The *Observer*, for instance, pointed out that the labor troubles in South Carolina had mostly ended peaceably. The reason was, the *Observer* argued, that in Gastonia the strike leaders were "avowed communists and bolsheviks from outside," while in South Carolina, strike leaders were native southerners. "American methods are being used in South Carolina," the *Observer* concluded; "Russian methods at Gastonia."[24] Again and again, however, from the very beginning of the trouble in Gastonia, the *Observer* would blast the "Red Russians" and "foreign organizers" who provoked all the trouble.[25] The *Elizabethton Star* and the *Gastonia Daily Gazette* insisted just as vehemently on the "foreignness" of the labor leaders.

For opponents of the strikes, the metaphors of transgression and crime, violent eruption, foreign invasion, and war fluidly morphed into each other. Probably nowhere was this more apparent than in the furious editorials of David Clark, editor of the *Southern Textile Bulletin*. Prominent Charlotte citizen, entrepreneur, and journalist, Clark was a popular public speaker, a director of Rotary International, and perhaps the most widely consulted spokesman for textile management.[26]

To Clark, the tie between unions, communists, subversion, free-lovism, and Negro equality was entirely clear.

In an interview with the *Charlotte Observer*, Clark denounced the "communistic program of free love and inter-racial intercourse." The strike at Loray, he insisted

> was started by two boys and a girl, the oldest of whom is about 25 years of age, all of whom live in the North. They somewhere, probably in school or college, came under the influence of radicals and communists, and affiliated themselves with the Young Communists, which is a branch of the I.W.W. They profess to believe that Russia, with its socialism, social equality, free love, and atheism, is a heaven into which all workers should enter.

The strike itself attracted mostly "boys and girls," who, "being young . . . were easily led into disorders." Clark was especially infuriated by the NTWU's call for racial equality within the union: " Their demand that negroes be admitted to the union on an equal basis with whites is in keeping with an editorial in their official organ, the *Daily Worker* . . . on March 29, 1929, which . . . insisted upon white girls dancing with negro men 'to break down capital-instilled prejudices.'"[27] Although the *Bulletin* ascribed these "rotten" ideas to communists, it insisted that all trade-unionists endorsed them. In fact, the *Bulletin* argued, there wasn't a dime's worth of difference between the United Textile Workers organizers and the communists; all trade-unionists were criminals.[28]

Military metaphors appeared in multiple guises in the press because they were used in multiple ways. Military imagery, for example, was as prevalent among the strikers themselves as among their opponents.

Historians have long argued that The Great War had a tremendous impact on American life and on the American South. Having rallied to fight for democracy abroad, American workers genuinely wanted to fight for industrial democracy at home. According to historian Joseph McCartin, this call for industrial democracy could be found among workers across the nation. Reporters heard it frequently in the thousands of little mill towns that dotted the industrial South.[29]

The economic impact of the war on textile country was enormous. The war triggered a huge explosion in demand; the cotton mills couldn't produce cloth fast enough. Mountains of uniforms, blankets, tents, socks, and who knows how many other textile products had to be produced, not just for American soldiers, but for armies around the world. Then came the crash. After 1919 demand plunged. Government orders went down and even worse, women's skirt lengths went up. As hemlines ascended, demand for cloth plunged. All through the 1920s the badly over-expanded textile industry struggled, unsuccessfully, to climb back up from the postwar decline.[30]

The Great War's significance went far beyond demand and supply, however. The war uprooted mill hill boys and shipped them all over the United States and all over the world. It wasn't easy to get the boys back in the mills after they'd seen Paree. The mill boys had had experiences their parents hadn't, and so had their sisters, many of whom had enthusiastically contributed to the war effort. Parents compared the mills to life on the played-out red-clay dirt farms, and found them good. Their children compared their lives in the mills to life in the wider nation and even the wider world, and found them wanting.[31]

The war's most powerful impact was on self-perceptions and values, and its impact was present everywhere. That certainly is what struck Anne O'Hare McCormick. Writing about the South for the *New York Times* in 1930, McCormick visited some of the old World War I training camps, and wrote:

> Go to any Southern town near a training camp and see what has happened to it since young men from all parts of the country mingled here. The merchants will tell you that "since the war" there is demand for a kind and variety of goods they never carried before. The preachers will tell you that their flocks are diminished and more worldly-minded. The planters and manufacturers will say that the working population is restless and independent, the labor turnover doubled or tripled.[32]

American wartime patriotism had taken on a decidedly ideological, rather than ethnic, tone. Unlike the French or Italians or Germans who appealed to ethnic solidarity, Americans appealed to a shared set of democratic ideals. America became the "arsenal of democracy," and the war itself was portrayed as a defense of democracy against militarism and tyranny. Some people, out on the mill hills, took all this democratic rhetoric seriously, and wondered whether it applied to them, too.

Reporters were struck by the sight in Elizabethton, for example, of workers parading down Elk Avenue behind flapping American flags; many of the men wore their old uniforms. The fact that Bemberg-Glanzstoff was a German-owned and -managed firm helped revive memories of the war against the Kaiser. Surveyor U. G. Ellis's remark at an Elizabethton union rally, "the men of Carter County had broken the Hindenburg Line, which they claimed could not be broken, and I hope that you stick together and break the Mothwurf Line!" reported in the *Star*,[33] explicitly linked management with the wicked Kaiser while linking the strikers with the heroic doughboys of the Great War.

Some of the young women in Elizabethton used flags both to assert their right to full citizenship and to provoke their more conservative onlookers. Jacqueline Dowd Hall writes that during one of the trials in Elizabethton striker Trixie Perry took the stand in a dress sewn from red, white, and blue bunting and a cap made of a small American flag. The prosecuting attorney began his cross-examination:

"You have a United States flag as a cap on your head?"
"Yes."
"Wear it all the time?"
"Whenever I take a notion."
"You are dressed in a United States flag . . .?"
"I guess so, I was born under it, guess I have a right to."[34]

Later in 1929, in the Marion strike, a "flying squad" of strikers all dressed in their old army uniforms and rushed out to the picket lines. Most were veterans of North Carolina's 81st Infantry Division, and they called themselves the "Wildcat Gang."[35]

Toward the end of Myra Page's strike novel, *Gathering Storm*, a millhand bitterly complains that he had gone off to fight for democracy in the Great War, only to come home to the oppression of the mill village. He shows a ragged scar to a coworker and says, "that's what I got, fightin' for democracy. Wal, us on the mill hills ain't seen on sliver of that thar democracy we heerd so much about a few years aback. . . . This strike is aimin' at gettin' some of what we was promised, back thar in '17."[36]

The long season of violence, reported so faithfully in the papers, conjured up images of its own antithesis. For example, the long strike in Danville broke out in September 1930. The strike dragged on, week after weary week, into the winter; it wouldn't end until January 1931.

Winters can get very cold in the little towns in south central Virginia, and it snowed in Danville on December 17. It was, according to the *Richmond Times-Dispatch* reporter, "the worst snowstorm Danville has had in twelve years [and] it came as a flank attack today on the Danville textile strikers and brought with it greater misery than that hitherto endured with fortitude by the rank and file of the workers." Pickets shivered on the line outside the mills, evicted families froze in makeshift housing, people were hungry, people were cold.[37]

This is not the image the *Danville Register* conveyed, however. Wearied by all the turmoil in its town, the *Register* saw something quite different. "Main Street," the *Register* reported the next day,

presented a beautiful appearance last night far exceeding any artist's portrayal of a Christmas scene. With snow banked five and six feet high in many places, and pedestrians slipping and sliding on the slick walkways, many colored lights strung on the Christmas trees that line the sidewalks transformed the usually drab business thoroughfare into a vision of transcendent loveliness.[38]

Such visions of transcendent loveliness encouraged an intense nostalgia that mightily played into management's hands. Newspapers frequently recollected the peaceful times before the strikes, times when, presumably, everyone cooperated, everyone was happy. The press often used this rupture of time into a prosperous and jovial "pre-strike" time, and a violent and acrimonious "strike time" to argue, strangely for papers utterly wedded to economic progress, that, as the *Elizabethton Star* had said from the very beginning, the past was better than the present, that change meant turmoil, that management stood for peace and law and unions stood for anarchy and pain. As the *Charlotte News* insisted in an editorial of the same name, "everybody loses in a strike."[39] In a bitter editorial, quite similar in tone to the *Gastonia Gazette*, the *Charlotte News* denounced Albert Weisbord and the Gastonia Reds: "His remarks sound like the raving of some sort of maniac. In all of his rambling sentences, there is not a suggestion of logic or reason; the whole tone of his tirade is to engender bitterness in the hearts of these people he hopes are ignorant enough not to know any better." The *News* then distinguished between the good past and the wicked present: "This whole trouble . . . is the result of these imported agitators. We were getting along peacefully down here until it occurred to these communistic leaders that the South would be a fine place for them to do fancy financial picking in and down they have swooped upon us." Finally, based on this argument, the *News* called for the restoration of the natural order of things, in which workers wishing for help applied where they ought, to the owners of capital:

We doubt not that the mill workers do have some grievances . . . [but] . . . the South is not going to tolerate the sowing of the seed of Communism in this territory. There is no section of the United States where such a spirit and such a doctrine are held in greater contumely than right here and if the mill workers really want succor, they will have to sever their relations with these fanatical leaders and do business through their own folks, with those who are in control of the manufacturing plants.[40]

This image of what happened lasted a long time. In 1946 Gaston County celebrated its centennial. Its souvenir program included a very brief comment about the 1929 strike. "Hard on the heels of the textile boom in Gaston County," the program explained, "came the labor unions, sending many fiery workers into the state, and county, and neighboring states, and making of a peaceful section a hotbed of hatred and strife.”[41]

Violent struggle was the most obvious dimension of the strikes reflected in the news reports, and often mixed metaphors of struggle are typical of the reporters' dispatches. More often than not, their stories relate how the tragic invaded the pastoral, how outside agitators exploded happy communities. Behind and within this surface violence were the strikers themselves, people quite unfamiliar not only to reporters but to most of the middle-class South. Who were these people? Like ethnographers, it was up to the reporters to shape an identity for these strange people who had so suddenly exploded into the public sphere and onto the newspapers' front pages.

NOTES

1. “Women Take Active Part,” *CO*, April 3, 1929, 3.
2. “Strike Threat Hangs Over Two Counties,” *CN*, April 7, 1929, 1.
3. Buch, *A Radical Life*, 219.
4. “Troops from Charlotte . . . ,”*CO*, April 3, 1929, 1.
5. “Communists Threaten . . . ,” *CO*, April 4, 1929, 1.
6. “Strike Threat Hangs Over Two Counties,” *CN*, April 7, 1929, 1; “Quite Prevails in Loray Strike Situation — Over Two Hundred Guardsmen Keep Grim Watch As Strikers Threaten Loray Mill . . . ,” *CN*, April 4, 1929, 1; “Union Threatens Strike in Charlotte Mill,” *CN*, April 5, 1929, 1; “Hint Strike Threatens High Shoals Mill Today,” *CN*, April 10, 1929, 1; “New Menace Feared in Loray Strike Situation — Crowd Gave Fiery Talk Big Ovation, Police Told,” *CN*, April 14, 1929, 1.
7. “No Troops at Danville,” *RT-D*, October 21, 1930, 10.
8. “Troops at Danville” (editorial), *RT-D*, November 27, 1930, 6; also “Cool Heads at Danville” (editorial), *RT-D*, November 29, 1930, 6.
9. “The Shooting at Schoolfield,” *DR* (editorial), December 12, 1930, 4.
10. “Officers Use Bayonets and Blackjacks to Stop Gastonia Strike Parade,” *RNO*, April 23, 1929, 1; “Scenes in ‘War’ on Gastonia's Street Told By Correspondent,” *CO*, April 23, 1929, 18; “Officers Again Break Up Gastonia Strike Parade,” *RNO*, April 24, 1929, 1.
11. Telegram from Charles Wood to Hugh Kerwin, April 22, 1929, Labor Conciliation Service, NA RG 280 170-4904.
12. “Lawlessness By Law Enforcers” (editorial), *CN*, April 23, 1929, 8.
13. “Deputies Halt Parade Staged with Disorder,” *CO*, April 23, 1929, 1.
14. Wilber Cash would argue in *The Mind of the South* that in many ways it was the “respectable people” who were ultimately responsible for the “mob,” at least in the sense that mob behavior was ultimately in their interests. Earlier, Mary Vorse made a similar claim in her Gastonia novel, *Strike!,* in which she insists that the real home of the “mob” was in the finer homes in the better neighborhoods. In fact, the link between the “better classes” and terrorist mobs became quite clear as early as the outbreak of Ku Klux Klan terrorism in the 1870s; see Eric Foner's research, cited in Paul D. Escott and David R. Goldfield, ed., *Major Problems in the History of the American South*, Vol. II (New York: Heath, 1990), 60–61.
15. “First Violence . . . ,” *DR*, September 24, 1930, 1.

16. "Textile Strike hits Woodruff," *CO*, Tuesday, April 2, 1929, 3; also, "Loray Mill Runs at Half Capacity," *RNO*, April 3, 1929, 1.

17. "Textile Mill Officials . . . ," *CN*, April 7, 1929, 18.

18. "Troops Ready as Tennessee Mills Prepare to Reopen," *CO*, May 6, 1929, 1.

19. "War is on at Elizabethton," *CO*, May 9, 1929, 7.

20. "Woman Ends Strike in Tennessee Mills," *NYT*, May 26, 1929, 1.

21. "Quite Prevails . . . ," *CN*, April 4, 1929, 1.

22. "Marion Sheriff Held on Murder Charges," *NYT*, October 4, 1929, 1; "An Evil Portent" (editorial), *GP*, September 12, 1929, 4; Forest Bailey, "Gastonia Goes on Trial," *The New Republic*, April 7, 1929, 332–34; "Class War in North Carolina," *The New Republic*, September 25, 1929, 321–22.

23. "IWW-ism Arrives" (editorial), *CO*, April 4, 1929, 8.

24. "The Difference" (editorial), *CO*, April 7, 1929, 8.

25. For instance, see: "An Impossible Strike" (editorial), *CO*, April 5, 1929, 8; "Loray Strike Condemned by U.S. Agent," *CO*, April 6, 1929, 1; "Strike Alarms Chief Metts," *CO*, April 6, 1929, 1.

26. He was elected in the summer of 1929; see "David Clark Elected Director of Rotary International," *STB*, June 13, 1929, 23.

27. "Clark Scouts Importance of Youth's Strike at Gastonia: Publisher declares Communistic Program of Free Love and Inter-Racial Intercourse Misses Fire," *CO*, April 6, 1929, 1. The "two boys and a girl" probably are Beal, Pershing, and Vera Buch. Clark is mistaken, of course, to think that the "Young Communists" are part of the I.W.W. See also: "Communists Threaten Sweeping Textile Strike," *CO*, April 5, 1929, 1; "Will Workers Stand for It?" (editorial), *CO*, April 18, 1929, 8; "Will They Accept Negroes?" (editorial), *CO*, May 14, 1929, 8.

28. "What Difference?" *STB*, October 3, 1929, 24.

29. Joseph A. McCartin, *Labor's Great War. The Struggle for Industrial Democracy and, the Origins of Modern American Labor Relations 1919–1921* (Chapel Hill: University of North Carolina, 1997). See, in particular, McCartin's discussion of the United Textile Workers (166–71), as well as his discussion of southern politicians (184–86).

30. On the troubles in textiles see: Claudius T. Murchison, *King Cotton is Sick* (Chapel Hill: University of North Carolina, 1930); Nancy Frances Kane, *Textiles in Transition: Technology, Wages, and Industry Relocation in the U.S. Textile Industry, 1880–1930* (Westport, Connecticut: Greenwood Press, 1988).

31. Hall, "Women," 367. For a detailed study of the impact of the Great War on America's working women, see Maurine Weiner Greenwald, *Women, War, and Work* (Ithaca: Cornell University Press, 1980).

32. Anne O'Hare McCormick, "The South: Its Second Reconstruction," *NYT*, June 8, 1930, V, 4.

33. "Kelly Appeals to Head of Federation," *ES*, May 8, 1929, 1; see Hall's comments, as well, in "Women," 366–67.

34. Hall, "Women," 373; Hall and her colleagues in *Family* note that textile workers were "emboldened by the democratic rhetoric of the Great War;" see Hall, *Family*, 184. The Great War's impact on democratic consciousness was hardly unique to textile workers. See, for instance, David Corbin's discussion of the same phenomenon among coal miners, in David

Alan Corbin, *Life, Work, and Rebellion in the Coal Fields* (Urbana: University of Illinois, 1981), 189.

35. See “Troops Quell Riot at Southern Mill,” *NYT*, August 20, 1929, 3.

36. Myra Page, *Gathering Storm* (New York: International Publishers, 1932), 294.

37. “Snow Causes Added Misery in Strike Area,” *RTD*, December 18, 1930, 1.

38. “Main St. Now Scene of Beauty,” *DR*, December 18, 1930, 1.

39. “Everybody Loses . . .” (editorial), *CN*, April 5, 1929, 8.

40. “A Gutterful of Abuse” (editorial), *CN*, April 9, 1929, 8.

41. Gaston County Centennial Committee, *Gaston Centennial (1846–1946), Souvenir Program* (Gastonia, 1946), Gaston County Public Library.

4

Portraits of Workers

When Fred Beal, the communist strike leader in Gastonia, first arrived in Charlotte in January 1929, he hurried off to see the city's lonely communist, whom Beal called "Tom King." King, who was blind, called on his son, Henry, to lead Beal and a friend off to Charlotte's mill village community. It was getting dark, Beal remembered. He asked Henry King where they were going and how they'd be able to identify the millhands. "Heavens," young Henry laughed, "you'll have no trouble picking out a textile worker from a human being."[1]

Apocryphal or not, young Henry's remark encapsulates a fundamental reality about life in the textile South. Respectable southerners were of two very different minds about the thousands of mills that peppered the Piedmont by the beginning of the turn of the twentieth century. Everyone was obsessed with industrial progress, true, but, as historian David Carleton writes, "the enormous expansion of the mill population, especially around the towns, was seen as the injection of a new and dangerous element into community life."[2] By the early twentieth century, there were all sorts of efforts to improve the mill villages, to clean them up, and to discipline their inhabitants. "The response of the 'town people' to what they termed the 'mill problem,'" Carleton writes "was to seek ever greater control over the operatives."[3] Mill owners' "paternalism," the intrusive management style so characteristic of mill owners, evolved in part as an exercise in social control. In the South in the 1920s, millhands were a group apart, isolated in their mill villages, unknown to the respectable South, thought of, more often than not, virtually in racial terms as a different breed, puzzled about as if they were exotics, worried over as if they were primitives.

Lois MacDonald was a preacher's daughter, born in 1897, who grew up in a mill town in South Carolina (and who would later become an important social reformer in the South). When she was a child, she would later recall,

On Saturday afternoon, you'd go uptown and you would see mill people — most of them would still have their overalls on — and they'd have little specks of lint, sometimes even on their hair. And I remember we used to say they all looked sick. They looked kind of pasty-faced. And between the town and the mill people there was a great gulf. They lived in a typical mill village, and in those days . . . I'm sure there were no facilities. I guess there was a church down there. But if you lived on the mill hill, you belonged up there. And there was no social contact in those days.[4]

Marion mill hands, according to historian Sam Howie, repeatedly noted in later interviews that mill work seemed to carry with it a kind of "disgrace," that workers were often dismissed by their white fellow citizens as "trash." Workers, Howie writes "commented at length on the fact that . . . mill workers were not looked upon as Marion's most outstanding citizens . . . [they were called] 'lintheads' by townspeople, a term which carried with it a reputation for excessive drinking, broken families, and juvenile delinquency."[5]

Ada Wilson, who was twenty-six in 1929 and worked in Charlotte, commented too about the enormous gap between millhands and townspeople: "We was 'trash' out here; we was 'poor white trash' because we worked in the mill [laughter], . . . I never did know anybody much outside this district."[6]

Northern reporters who flocked south to cover the strikes were fascinated by the millhands. Describing the workers' habits and habitats, though, proved to be an unusually difficult task.

The mill villages were one of the first things that caught reporter Anne O'Hare McCormick's eye as she toured the South in 1930. "Mills and mill villages," she wrote for the *New York Times*, "spread like ragged spider webs around new textile centers — Charlotte, Greenville, Greensboro, Spartanburg — or are spotted singly along the red uplands of the Piedmont, as cloistered and self-centered as walled towns in the Middle Ages." They were, she wrote, "as distinctive on the Southern scene as the live oak. . . . The worst are huddles of sad shacks on ravaged hillsides, or shacks wobbling on stilts in red clay; the best are suburban developments in the modern manner, prim cottages set behind hedges on curving roads, paved and landscaped."[7]

Overall, she was impressed by them. The villages, she reported, provided cheap housing and often decent schools, hospitals, and even recreation centers. "I do not know which would be more shocked," she added, "the Southern mill owners or the Communists, to hear that I was continually reminded of Russia as I was shown the excellent welfare schemes in the mill villages." The villages, she continued, "are all alike in this: no matter how happily they are planned or how carefully they are planted and kept in repair by the owner, they look like temporary abiding places. The houses are not homes. They go with the job and belong to the mill. Moreover, they make the worker belong to the mill as he could not by the mere fact of employment alone." As for the mill villagers, McCormick concluded, "they are hardly citizens at all; they are physically segregated and socially ostracized, nearly a million people all told, 'economic units' in a very literal sense."[8]

She was struck by the contradictions embedded in the mill village. The "mill village," she wrote, "the plantation of the cotton mill [was] also a feudal institution, often benevolent, necessary to the establishment of the textile industry in a wholly rural environment, but out of place in a democracy and out of date in a modern industrial system."[9]

Historian Douglas Flamming notes that in times of labor shortages, southern mill owners had to provide decent housing and facilities if they wanted to attract labor, and that in some ways these company towns were thus, in a sense, achievements of labor.[10] It was sometimes hard for workers to see the towns as their own, however. Hattie Hylton, for example, the director of welfare work in the Riverside and Dan River Mill's village in Danville, complained in 1915 at a conference of mill village welfare workers about her millhands' lackadaisical ways. She had started a "civic league" in the Schoolfield mill village, she explained, and the civic league had sponsored contests for the best lawn and tidiest house in the mill village, but alas, the millhands weren't much interested. "We expect this interest to be very gradual," she explained,

> because of the perfect indifference on the part of many of the people to the improvement of anything that belongs to the mill — they say "If the mill wants it done, let 'em do it themselves." Our League leaders are those who have none of this spirit and they can combat it better than anyone else can because they are of the people. Our village drug store has increased its sale of garden seeds one hundred percent in the last two years of the League's existence. We are sure we can see that our work is gradually bringing about a higher degree of efficiency on the part of the employees, and it seems hardly too much to hope that it will finally break down and dispel the stigma which has so long been attached to cotton mills and their operatives.[11]

To the Yankee reporters, the mill villages were odd and strange places. Louis Stark was one of The *New York Times*'s best-known labor reporters; his stories appeared not only in the *Times* but in dozens of other papers. What impressed Stark was that for most millhands, the mill village was a kind of trap: "The charge leveled against the mill village is that it does not provide for training its children to enter work outside the mills. Conditions are such that there is nothing for the grown child to do but to enter the mill. Once employed in the mill his income is so low and his leisure so short that he is unable to find time or money to prepare himself for another occupation."[12]

"What most strikes the explorer in the cotton country," Anne O'Hare McCormick wrote in The *New York Times* in 1930, "is that it makes so many poor and so few rich."[13]

The reporters' biggest challenge in the strike years would be to paint a portrait of these many poor. Even for people who knew them well, they would be hard to capture in words.

Harriot Herring was a frequent visitor to the trial of the Gastonia Seven in Charlotte. Herring was a social worker who had spent most of her life working in the Piedmont's mill villages. Few people knew millhands better than Herring. From New York, Beulah Amidon, editor of The *Survey*, had written Herring and asked for her impressions. In August Herring wrote Amidon that Judge Barnhill impressed her by his fairness. She had some passing comments about the lawyers, but what really impressed her was the crowd:

The people who crowded the courtroom were obviously working people — cotton mill people, some in their Sunday clothes, but many in their overalls. . . . The crowd there was quiet, almost stolid in impassivity. . . . Some of the people I talked to in the audience said that the only folks sticking by the union and the strike were the "rakings and scrapings". . . . But certainly the friends of the accused are not that type. . . . They were as upstanding, vigorous and intelligent as any in the room.[14]

Later she would add:

I sat in at the Aderholt trial . . . where the courtroom was filled with workers. It was obvious to anyone watching their faces that they were almost to a man in favor of the defendants. I talked to many of them as I sat beside them or as I met them in the lobby. Everyone was for the strikers and assured me that all the workers they knew were also for them and for the union. "It looks like the working people have got to get together. They can't live as things are now" — such was the conclusion of one after another. . . . They didn't seem to be bothering much about the issues of communism or social equality of the Negro. It was the union as an economic tool.[15]

T. S. Matthews covered the trial of the Gastonia Seven for *The New Republic*. One of his reports begins by taking the reader into the courthouse:

As you approach the Mecklenburg County Courthouse, a great white stone building with classical facade and a long sweep of steps, you pass a granite obelisk dedicated to the "Mecklenburg Signers of the Declaration of Independence." On one side of the this shaft a brass plaque has been set into the stone, representing a hornet's nest, with the inscription across it, "Let Us Alone."

The courtroom itself, Matthews reported, "is large and airy, pleasantly lighted by huge windows." He was more impressed by the crowds, however, dressed, some of them, in the "unalterable Southern farmer's uniform of overalls, blue shirt, and black slouch hat." He added, a bit dreamily, "looking at them, you see the same faces, the same clothes, almost, of the men who marched with Stonewall Jackson and Longstreet, and raided with Jubal Early." Inside the courthouse the crowds were thick, and the air was "reeking with cigar-smoke and that air of affable venality that pervades our public buildings." Even here, it was the men in overalls that struck him most: "here too, shuffling down the marble corridors, hawking expertly into the brass spittoons, and bending rather shamefacedly over such a modern contraption as the drinking fountains, the faded blue overalls and the black slouch hats wander or stand patiently, leaning against the polished walls."[16]

Matthews' report merges, confusingly, several different images. The millhands first emerge as strong figures, as romantic Confederate soldiers. Then they fade out as Matthews' condescension grows, disappearing as persons, merging instead with their own symbols, skin and bone fading into faded blue overalls and black slouch hats.

Louis Stark, the *New York Times* reporter, also wrote for the *New Republic*. In the spring of 1929, just after the strikes broke out, Stark published an article there ambitiously titled, "The Meaning of the Textile Strike."[17] In it he followed one "strand in the [textile] network," to the little town of Pineville, North Carolina, some ten miles south of Charlotte: "a typical, semi-isolated mill village, Pineville is a group of shabby, box-like bungalows on stilts. The boxes form an arc above and beyond the mill. A straggling, red dirt road leads from one end of the arc to the mill. Through the fields and 'up the hill' is a tortuous path winding lazily to the other end of the arc."[18]

There, in Pineville's mill village, Stark met "Alfred E."

Stark described Alfred E. as "a tall, loose-jointed" man, "slow of gait and speech." Alfred E.'s face "is sunken and filled with a criss-cross of lines. A three days' stubble is on his chin. He says he is thirty-eight years old but looks much older."[19]

Alfred E. was on strike. For the first time in his life. He had worked in the mills since he was a child and had married a girl from the mills. They had three babies and then she died. Things had gotten very hard. He earned around $22.50 per week, or around $1170 per year. The mill owners then announced the "stretch out." More work was to be required per worker, and the net effect was to cut Alfred E.'s pay by 24 percent, down to $17 per week, or around $884 per year. He and his babies simply couldn't survive on that.

Stark noted that in Massachusetts in the late 1920s millhands worked a forty-eight-hour week, while southern millhands worked a fifty-five hour week, but southern workers were paid around 16.3 percent less than northern workers.

Wasn't the cost of living cheaper in the South? Elsewhere Stark had addressed that issue. The National Industrial Conference Board, he reported, conducted a study in 1919–20, comparing the annual cost of living in Fall River, Massachusetts to that in Pelzer, South Carolina. The results were:

	Fall River	Pelzer
food	$572	709.80
shelter	117	48
clothing	243.36	278.57
heat, light, fuel	70.20	78.24
sundries	265.20	259.48
total	1267.76	1374.09

In fact, the annual cost of living was actually slightly higher in the South than in the North, yet southern workers were paid substantially less.[20]

Alfred E. fed his children on bread, molasses, and sometimes vegetables. Milk and butter were too expensive. There were no relatives to help out. At five a.m. each day he arose and got to the mill before the six a.m. shift whistle blew. He worked twelve-hour shifts. The oldest of the children cared for the two little ones while their daddy worked in the mill.

Alfred E., Stark wrote,

> is proud of his "pure Anglo-Saxon blood." He ought to be, for the politicians remind him of it very often. They urge Alfred to be on his guard against "the agitator who would tear down our noble institutions in the dust." Alfred used to applaud these patriotic sentiments. But that was before the mills installed stop-watches, time studies, and various concomitants of the efficiency system. Recently, however, he listened to one of the agitators who came over from Gastonia. She promised him the support of "a powerful union" if he went on strike. Alfred reasoned that he had nothing to lose. He joined the strike.[21]

And, Stark concluded,

> the Alfreds, their wives and children, about 15,000 in all, went on strike recently in ten mills in the Carolinas and two in Tennessee. The strikes came without warning and were a distinct shock to the communities. They brought with them the biggest labor troubles since the Charlotte strike of 1921. The spark that set off the conflagration was applied by the National Textile Workers Union.[22]

"Robert C." was another of Stark's archetypical images of the southern worker. Reporting on Elizabethton, what struck Stark most was the "new kind of Southern hillman" he encountered. The mountaineers had been wooed to the mills by impressive propaganda, glossy photographs of all the modern things they would be able to buy with their factory wages, and, Stark said, "the glowing pictures had the desired effect on the simple folk." Reality had shattered illusion, however, and so out on strike they went. "And a strange strike it was," Stark wrote. "Lean, sinewy mountaineers, with their wives and children, perhaps the most individualistic people in the United States, were urged to meet industrialization by unionizing."

People who, Stark thought, were remarkably "clannish" and suspicious of foreigners forged a massive collective effort overnight. Elizabethton's "Tabernacle," Stark reported, used by the union for its strike rallies, was a "rude structure of boards, with floor of tarbark;" it was routinely jammed with thousands of mountaineers and their families. "The aisles were crowded and boys hung from the rafters."

The men, Stark continued, "run to the tall, rangy type, spare and lithe, and the women are sturdy and dignified." They reminded Stark of images of the Revolutionary War, when mountaineers had come down from the hills to fight the king.

Robert C. was one of them. He was twenty-nine, married, and the father of three children. He and his wife lived with his widowed mother, his sister, and his sisters' three children. He had no education to speak of. He had worked in the mills for two years; he worked a fifty-six-hour week at $0.40 an hour, or about $22.40 per week. He couldn't get by on what he made, Stark wrote. He wanted better for his children than what he had, he didn't want them to have to go to the mills, but he had no hope for them unless things changed. Robert C. was an angry man, and, Stark reported, he is also heavily armed.[23]

Alfred E. and Robert C. were, of course, attempts to humanize the strikers, to translate them, via synecdoche, from category to person. Alfred E. and Robert C. were not exactly persons either, they were archetypes. As archetypes, they reflected not only reporters' idiosyncrasies, but deeply embedded cultural metaphors.

Reporters like Stark, who were obviously sympathetic to the strikers, typically portrayed them as American versions of noble savages. Rude and uncouth they may have been, but they were rude and uncouth in the tradition of Daniel Boone and Davy Crockett. Stark's Alfred E. was "a tall, loose-jointed" man, "slow of gait and speech;" Robert C. was a "lean, sinewy" mountaineer. Stark explicitly evoked images of the over-the-mountain pioneers of the Revolutionary War. Consider an early *New York Times* report, possibly written by Stark, that recounted a visit to Elizabethton by the AFL's president William Green, shortly after the botched kidnapping of the United Textile Workers' organizers. "From a platform in a rude tabernacle in Happy Valley, hemmed in by the Great Smokies on one side and the Cumberland Mountains on the other," the report began, AFL President William Green spoke to Elizabethton's millhands. While he spoke, "young, soft-voiced mountaineers from Stony Creek, whose contact with industrial civilization is as recent and fresh as the blooming redbud and dogwood on the slopes of Happy Valley, guarded all approaches to the house occupied by the two labor leaders (Hoffmann and McGrady), whose rooms were veritable arsenals of Winchesters."[24]

Stark's reporting reflected, and perhaps inspired, a widespread northern liberal explanation of the southern strikes. As the *New York Times* editorialized, the millhands were not a modern industrial working class at all, but were, rather, a kind of pre-industrial folk who simply were not yet used to the rigors of industrial life. Nor were the mill managers used to modern industrial ways. By implication, the *Times* argued that with maturity, the mill owners would learn modern management techniques, and millhands would calm down. What was going on then was more like a peasant rebellion than a class war. As the peasants modernized and fit better into the industrial order, they would, presumably, abandon their militancy.[25]

Stark's romantic image of the millhands, carried on the *Times*'s front page and widely syndicated in other papers — his portrait of them virtually in buckskin and 'coonskin caps — was thus more than simple reportage. It was a reflection of a specific type of analysis of what was happening in the mill towns. How much that analysis had to do with the realities of the millhands' lives is another story.

Certainly many southern reporters would question whether northern reporters got the story right. The editors of the *Charlotte News* were furious at what they thought were "grotesque and absurd" portraits of southern millhands. Commenting on demands for a U.S. Senate hearing on the South's textile industry, the *News* insisted that the South had nothing to fear from such an investigation, nothing except for yankee bile.[26] While northern reports tended to paint generally sympathetic portraits of the millhands, southern reports were much more complex.

What were the mill villages like? Southern papers insisted, with few exceptions, that the mill villages were, all in all, fine places in which to live. During the trouble in Gastonia, a Loray mill official drove a reporter from the *Charlotte Observer* through one of the Loray villages, and she spotted "scores of very nice, comfortable-looking homes," each rented, the official pointed out, for a mere fifty cents per week. The only complaint the reporter had was that there wasn't much grass or shrubbery around them.[27]

What about the millhands themselves? The *Southern Textile Bulletin* insisted that the South's millhands were an exuberant lot. Quoting the *Spartanburg Herald*, the *Bulletin* noted in early January 1929 that "the people in the textile . . . communities are enjoying this Christmas more than any in years. . . . The social gatherings at the mills during the holidays are proving quite popular."[28] Almost every issue of the *Bulletin* included a "home section" edited by "Becky Ann," a pseudonym for the extremely popular writer Ethel Thomas. The "home section" included letters about jolly events in this mill village and that, marriages and Christmas parties and funny things that happened at work. Thomas wrote a score of mill village novels. *Only A Factory Boy*, *Hearts of Gold*, and *Will Allen—A Sinner*, were some of her titles. They were all heart-warming stories of young romance and family affection among the power looms. Printed on cheap paper, sold for less than a dollar, and distributed by the mill owners, they were ubiquitous; tattered copies of Thomas's latest story circulated from one end of the Piedmont to the other. No one was very unhappy for long in the world Becky Ann painted.

In the spring of 1929, Becky Ann visited Gastonia. Although Becky Ann never talked politics, in this case she made an exception. "It breaks my heart to see them get into trouble such as Beal and Pershing are leading them into," she wrote of the millhands. "How our good mill people can be led by these people who are not our kind, who defy God, flout religion, denounce our government and who are working for social equality among white and black, is a mystery." It must be, Becky Ann concluded, that the millhands had somehow lost their senses. She was sure, though, that they'd come around.[29]

Pay was fair, housing was good, workers were happy. Workers enjoyed a "contented life," many of the southern papers claimed.[30] Thus, "there can be no question," the *Charlotte Observer* concluded, "that discontent has been stimulated by professional communistic and well-paid labor agitators."[31]

The image of the contented but dull-witted millhand, stirred to fury by outside agitators, could take newspapers in odd directions. For example, the *Charlotte News*, in an April 1929 editorial entitled "What is the Answer?" pointed out that workers were restless and upset. That they so easily followed Reds and trade-unionists was a "symptom" of a "lack of poise and balance and resistance" (note, of course, the implication that the workers were diseased). Then, shifting into a surprisingly "progressive" key, the editorial called not for more repression but for expanded education, "more and more education for the masses." Shifting again, the *News* switched to a deeply conservative tone. What education needed to teach the masses was that "life . . . is more than meat and the body more than raiment." Workers needed to learn to stop agitating for better conditions and wage increases; such demands reflect a crass "materialism" bred by ignorance, and "where there is paucity of education there is usually a slant toward the sheerest sort of materialism."[32]

At the same time, however, there was nothing simple about the southern papers' images of workers. Even as they explained just how happy the millhands were, the papers often included in their reports more than a little hostility toward the contented workers. To be sure, the newspapers rarely treated workers with outright contempt, although an undertone of contempt was not uncommon in news stories or in editor's comments.

In December 1929, for instance, the Johns Hopkins University Liberal Club invited David Clark, editor of the *Southern Textile Bulletin*, to come to Baltimore to debate Tom McMahon, president of the United Textile Workers. Clark was a thumb-in-the-eye sort of conservative; he had spent the past several months inveighing against trade unions in a most ferocious manner and had no intention of publicly debating Tom McMahon. "If you are fully informed as to Mr. McMahon's methods and records," he wrote the students, "you will appreciate further my objections to speaking with him." Anyway, Clark resented people from Maryland interfering in North Carolina's business. He sarcastically suggested that the Liberal Club investigate something closer to home, such as Maryland's own fish and fruit industries, and stay out of other states where they weren't welcome. If you look to your own affairs, Clark concluded, "you will not have much time in which to decide whether or not the people of North Carolina are proper guardians for the laboring people of North Carolina."[33]

It is curious but typical that Clark distinguished between the "people of North Carolina" and the "laboring people." It would appear that the two are both different and hierarchically ordered; after all, the "people" apparently have some sort of "guardian" role over the "laboring people." Even the word "guardian" is curious. Guardian can have positive connotations; immature children sometimes are cared for by "guardians." It can have negative connotations as well; prison inmates need guardians.

Richard Edmonds, editor of the *Manufacturers' Record*, was interviewed by a *Charlotte Observer* reporter when Edmonds was in Charlotte. Edmonds was predictably hostile to trade unions. He opposed any sort of collective bargaining. He boasted that if strikers didn't want their mill jobs, then owners would find plenty of people who did. Edmonds denied that workers had any genuine grievances. As for the strikers, Edmonds referred to them as the "worst class of labor." He had gone to Gastonia and had spoken with some of the strikers. "One," he told the reporter, "told me he'd just been released from an insane asylum. . . . Another, a woman, must have been vaccinated with a victrola needle, she had such a line of complaints." They were all, Edmonds concluded, from the "cesspool of humanity."[34]

The social gulf between respectable white southerners and the poor white millhands was enormous and more often than not assumed virtual caste proportions. One trigger for the strikes was workers' long-simmering rage at the social contempt they were forced to endure, and there is no denying the intensity of that contempt. Novelist Sherwood Anderson was not exaggerating when he insisted that to middle-class southerners, millhands were essentially "white niggers."[35]

Even "progressive" reporters shared this cruel class bias, and their fascination for H. L. Mencken only exacerbated it. Mencken had an enormous impact on young southern reporters like W. J. Cash and Gerald Johnson, and Mencken had very little faith in democracy. To him, the "common people" were so many fools, all potential members of the mob, who could be saved from themselves only by an enlightened elite. Both Cash and Johnson, sharp critics as they were of southern society, often lapsed into suspicion of or downright contempt for southern poor white millhands.[36]

In the papers the harshest language was reserved for Gastonia's communists; their speeches, for instance, were commonly described as "wild harangues."[37] Workers were often treated with a mocking condescension. They were foolish and easily misled; they had no thoughts of their own and simply parroted what the outside agitators told them to say. It was these outsiders, not the millhands, who made the strikes. A *Charlotte News* headline typified the papers' attitude: "'Foreign Agitators' Blamed for Textile Strike."[38]

Early in April 1929, for example, Vera Buch, Fred Beal, and several other Gastonia Reds drove over to nearby Pineville, south of Charlotte, to speak to striking workers there. The *Charlotte Observer* ran several stories about what happened. On April 9 a story entitled "'Beal Will Tell Us What It's All About,' Say Mill Workers" reported that none of the strikers had any idea what they were striking about. The story began:

> The sinister and yet magnetic and forceful figure of a youthful union organizer, preacher of communism, socialism, bolshevism and other assorted 'isms', follower of Karl Marx and successful collector of union initiation fees, is the only apparent reason for the strike down here in this peaceful little south Mecklenburg village. . . . "I don't know what we're striking about," is the way one young striker expressed it today. "Beal said he'd be back and tell us."

The report described the situation as "ludicrous."[39]

A story printed the next day took the same tone. Highlighting, as was typical, the violence associated with the strikes, the story was entitled "Disorders Mark the Second Day of Strike at Pineville Mill." In it the reporter laughed that "two union organizers, one a woman who has a clever command of the English in getting over her Russian propaganda . . . and a reporter who got hit with an egg, were stars today."[40]

For several decades the South's hometown newspapers had ignored the millhands, or complained about them, while insisting again and again that they were a fundamentally contented lot. None of these approaches helped reporters understand the workers' anger.

Millhands, before the 1920s, were not big newspaper readers, and of course they bought no advertising. Newspapers were neither written for them or about them. One can easily rummage through small-town papers year after year and find almost nothing about the millhands and their mill villages.

When a story did appear, it was likely to be critical. Especially around the turn of the century, when the mills were still new, they and their workers produced considerable alarm among the South's respectable classes, as David Carleton and others have demonstrated.

The fundamental position of virtually every southern paper, however, was that the millhands were a happy and contented class, thankful to their mill baron betters for their lot in life.

People flocked to the mills from played out farms because, the papers invariably argued, mill work was a step up in life. The *Charlotte Observer* conducted a study of mill workers' wages. Consider, the *Observer* calculated, that a farm family in North Carolina in 1929 would have an income of around $600 – $700 per year. Now, at the Loray Mill in Gastonia, a worker might make around $936 per year. If the husband, wife, and one child all worked at the mill, even if only one of them earned top wages, the mill family might well have a combined income of close to $2800 per year: "The income of the average family of textile workers in North Carolina is probably close to twice the income of the average farm family. . . . Textile workers . . . are not even the least fortunate class of our population in the matter of income." [41]

True, southern millhands earned less than northern millhands (this was the famous "wage differential" which made it attractive for northern mills to relocate south), but that wasn't really a hardship, the papers typically argued. The cost of living is lower in the South than in the North. Anyway, the papers continued, southern millhands got to live in the mill villages, company towns where rent was minimal and most amenities were provided at company expense. As for the mill village houses, why, the *Observer* argued, the "cottages are well built and in many cases have been praised for their beauty."[42]

What is curious in these reports is the undertone of exoticism they convey. The millhands, when they appear in the news reports in southern papers are described the way an anthropologist might describe some curious band of aborigines. For instance, were the strikers religious like most middle-class southerners were? The *Charlotte Observer* sent a reporter off to Gastonia to find out. No, she reported, in a front page story entitled "Mill Strikers Bother Little About Religion," they weren't very religious.[43]

The millhands were sexually suspect. One of the most frequently repeated charges made against the Gastonia Reds was that they preached "free love," and the papers warned that this insidious doctrine might well infect the workers. Indeed, one story warned that the Gastonia communists had urged women workers to seduce National Guardsmen.[44]

Yet southern papers often conveyed too a fundamental sympathy for the millhands. Generations of paternalism and white solidarity had imbued reporters and editors with a strong sense that "those people"— the strikers — were really "our people," a point papers made repeatedly. Even the most anti-union papers, such as the *Charlotte Observer* and the *Gastonia Daily Gazette*, expressed dismay at the site of arrested and evicted millhands. After the Gastonia strike had been broken, the *Gazette* even launched a fund-raising campaign to support workers who had been replaced by scabs. No doubt a publicity ploy by the paper, it also reflected the widespread concern for a restoration of harmony. It was this genuine concern for the workers that would drive the newspapers off into directions, explored in the chapters to follow, which few papers would have anticipated before the strikes.

In the end, however, one has the impression that neither the northern nor the southern reports could quite capture the millhands. At least some millhands were sure the reports written about them had very little to do with them. Throughout the strikes there was considerable tension between reporters and strikers. Reporters who hurried off to Greenville, South Carolina, to cover the strike there complained of being "accosted" by strikers,[45] and that was a common occurrence. In Pineville, strike leader Jess Smith angrily told the *Charlotte Observer*'s reporters: "No, we don't intend to give out a thing to the newspapers. . . . We don't like what the papers have written. Nothing they have printed is true, and we don't want to have anything to do with you and any of the others. That's all."[46]

NOTES

1. Beal, *Journey*, 112.

2. David L. Carleton, *Mill and Town in South Carolina, 1880–1920* (Baton Rouge: LSU Press, 1982), 146.

3. Carleton, *Town and Mill*, 10.

4. Interview with Lois MacDonald by Mary Frederickson, 1977, SOHP, SHC, UNC-CH, 4007-G-36; see also an earlier interview: Interview with Lois MacDonald by Marion Roydhouse, 1975, SOHP, SHC, UNC-CH, 4007-G-35.

5. Sam Watson Howie, *The New South in the North Carolina Foothills: A Study of the Early Industrial Experience in McDowell County*, Masters Thesis, Appalachian State University, 1976, 49.

6. Interview with Ada Wilson by Allen Tullos (1980), SOHP, SCH, UNC-CH, 4007-H-183.

7. Anne O'Hare McCormick, "The South: A Fabric of Cotton," *NYT*, June 1, 1930, V, 1.

8. Anne O'Hare McCormick, "The South: The New Labor and the Old," *NYT*, June 15, 1930, V, 8.

9. O'Hare McCormick, "The South," *NYT*, May 25, 1930, V, 1.

10. Flamming, *Creating*, especially Chapter 6.

11. "A Fifteen Minutes Talk On — The Schoolfield Welfare Work," by Miss Hattie E. Hylton, at the Welfare Conference of Southern Employers, Black Mountain, North Carolina, July 16, 1915, in Danville Public Library, Clippings, indexed by Clara G. Fountain, Vol, 8, 158–65.

12. Stark, "Textile Mill Troubles," *NYT*, May 19, 1929, X, 17.

13. Anne O'Hare McCormick, "The South: A Fabric of Cotton," *NYT*, June 1, 1930, V, 1.

14. Letter from Harriot Herring to Beulah Amidon, August 20, 1929, in Herring Papers.

15. Letter from Harriot Herring to Beulah Amidon, October 22, 1929, in Herring Papers, SHC, UNC-CH.

16. T. S. Matthews, "Gastonia in Court," *The New Republic*, September 18, 1929, 119–21.

17. Louis Stark, "The Meaning of the Textile Strike," *The New Republic*, May 8, 1929, 323–24.

18. Stark, "Meaning," 323.

19. Stark, "Meaning," 323.

20. Stark, "Textile Mill Troubles," *NYT*, May 19, 1929, X, 17.

21. Stark, "Meaning," 323.

22. Stark, "Meaning," 323.

23. "The Southern Hillman a New Kind of Striker," *NYT*, April 21, 1929, X, 7.

24. "Green Pledges Aid to Labor in South," *NYT*, April 8, 1929, 4.

25. "The Gastonia Mob" (editorial) *NYT*, September 11, 1929, 26. Commenting on the most recent violence in Gastonia, the *Times* editorialized: "the [difficulties] arise from the fact that the South has been newly industrialized and is in the midst of struggles over workers' claims which were fought out in other parts of the nation when smokestacks began building among the farms." Later, in "Rooted in the Soil" (editorial), *NYT*, September 9, 1929, 30, the *Times* described the continuing violence as the "growing pains of industrialization." The *Times* repeated the same point in "Order and Progress" (editorial), October 1, 1929, 30.

26. "Come Right Along Senator!" (editorial), *CN*, May 3, 1929, 8.

27. "Mill Strikers Bother Little About Religion," *CO*, April 8, 1929, 1.

28. "Mill People Enjoy Social Gatherings," *STB*, January 3, 1929, 11.

29. "Pictures Home Life in the Loray Community," *GDG*, April 12, 1929, 2; reprinted from the *STB*, April 11, 1929.

30. "IWW-ism Arrives" (editorial), *CO*, April 4, 1929, 8.

31. "Southern Labor" (editorial), *CO*, April 13, 1929, 8.

32. "What is the Answer?" (editorial), *CN*, April 12, 1929, 8.

33. Letter from David Clark to Joel Seidman, Johns Hopkins University Liberal Club, December 14, 1929, in Robert Cooke Papers, SHC, UNC-CH, 4715 - 1.

34. "*Manufacturers' Record* Editor Finds Mills Not Handicapped," *CO*, April 27, 1929, 1. The "cesspool" remark caused a lot of trouble. Edmonds insisted he had been misquoted; the reporter stood by the story. See: Letter from Richard Edmonds, *CO*, May 6, 1929, 8.

35. The white better classes "were always speaking of the ignorance and stupidity of the mill people," says the narrator in Sherwood Anderson's strike novel, *Beyond Desire* (New York: Liveright, 1932), 37. The protagonist of *Desire*, Red Oliver, is born and raised in a Georgia mill town. He is of lower middle-class, not really working-class background, but his widowed mother's poverty gradually plunges the Olivers downward in the class hierarchy.

His mother starts going to a "shouting Methodists'" church frequented by millhands. Red and his girlfriend (who happens to be the mill owner's daughter) pass by the church one Sunday. The young woman looks at the church, filled with enthusiastic white mill hands, smirks, and says: "like niggers." Oliver's hometown has two white baseball teams, one made up of men from the better classes, the other made up of millhands. They never play each other. The narrator remarks that "for the town team to have played the mill boys would have been almost like playing niggers. They wouldn't have said that, but they felt it" (39).

36. Gerald Johnson, for example, was deeply sympathetic to the millhands. He doubted that they, however, on their own, could accomplish much. Johnson's heroes were not the workers but middle-class reformers, like himself. See his essay "Service in the Cotton Mills," in Johnson, *South-Watching*, 64–71. Cash was in the habit of referring to millhands as "mill-peons."

37. "Few On Jobs During Night at Pineville," *CO*, April 9, 1929, 1.

38. "'Foreign Agitators' . . . ," *CN*, April 9, 1929, 1.

39. "'Beal Will Tell Us What It's All About,' Say Mill Workers," *CO*, April 9, 1929, 13.

40. "Disorders Mark Second Day of Strike at Pineville Mill," *CO*, April 10, 1929, 13.

41. "A Comparison" (editorial), *CO*, April 12, 1929, 8.

42. "Textile Workers' Wage in South Higher than in any other Zone, Survey Says," *CO*, April 23, 1929, 1.

43. "Mill Strikers Bother Little About Religion," by Cora Harris, *CO*, April 8, 1929, 1.

44. See: "Women Take Active Part in Gaston Mill Strike," *CO*, April 4, 1929, 3; "Agitators Appeal to Women in Spurring Gastonia Strike," *CO*, April 5, 1929, 14.

45. "Greenville Strikers Reject Offer," *CO*, April 4, 1929, 12. The strike ended after a week when management agreed to drop the hated stretch-out; see "Accord Gains at Greenville," *CO*, April 9, 1929, 2.

46. "Pineville Strikers Eager For Chance to Resume Work," *CO*, April 19, 1929, 14.

5

Girls Everywhere

When he heard the news about the trouble up in Elizabethton in the spring of 1929, novelist Sherwood Anderson hurried to the scene. As he talked with crowds of strikers picketing the Bemberg-Glanzstoff plants, what he noticed most were the women. Looking at the turmoil at union headquarters, for example, Anderson wrote for the *Nation*:

> Girls everywhere. What a different looking crowd from the one I saw, but two hours ago, coming from the factories. There was life in this crowd. . . . There is a report that the company is going to fire all those who join. "Well, then, we will go back to the hills. I lived on birdeye beans before there was any rayon plant and can live on birdeye beans again." At least there was joy in this room. Men and women, for the time at least, walked with new joy in their bodies. The men became more dignified, more manly in their bearing, the women more beautiful.[1]

Anderson guessed that three-fourths of the textile workers up in Elizabethton were women. He was wrong; women made up about 30 to 44 percent of the work force, but the very fact that Anderson's estimate was so skewed testifies not only to Anderson's poor arithmetic but to the powerful impact all the women made on him.[2] "They are," Anderson wrote,

> shockingly young. I saw many girls that could not have been beyond twelve or thirteen. In these towns, I am told, children have two ages, the real age and the "mill age." It is easy to escape responsibility. "If she lies about her age," etc. Of course she lies. These are the poorest of the poor people, from the hills, the mountain gullies. They went with weary steps along the road. Many of the young girls were already developing goiters, that sure sign of overwork, nervous debility. They had thin legs, stooped shoulders.[3]

When trouble broke out in Gastonia a month later, reporters were amazed, as Anderson had been, by the militancy of the mill women. By noon on April 1, according to one reporter, some fifty to sixty pickets, "composed very largely of boys and girls," had formed up outside the Loray mill gates.[4] It seemed to Legette Blythe, reporting for the *Charlotte Observer*, that in the first week of Gastonia's strike, perhaps half of the strikers, "were women and children. One woman carried a baby in one arm and a big knotted stick in the other. Another woman, apparently in her twenties, fought her way through the crowd to the front ranks of the strikers and shook a half-inch pipe at one of the guardsmen. She seemed in good humor, however, but she held on to the pipe."[5]

As she walked around the strike headquarters, *Observer* reporter Cora Harris was quite astonished by the numbers of women among the strikers. One woman worker was organizing a relief committee, other women were speakers at the seemingly interminable rallies. As in so many other strikes, these women made it a point to dress not in their work clothes, but in their respectable clothes. Many, that is, wanted to change from a costume that clearly marked them off as proletarians to a costume that stressed their role as respectable citizens. One afternoon, in blistering heat, Harris noticed many women "dressed in their gay Easter frocks and a few with spring coats. I was particularly attracted by the popularity of silk stockings."[6]

That the reporters should focus on the role of women in the strike is testimony to the reporters' accuracy. Women did, in fact, play a notable role in the strike wave. In Elizabethton Margaret Bowen had led the walkout and helped forge the union. Vera Buch, one of the yankees who was a key Gastonia strike leader, remembered that "a group of young women in their late teens, already workers for several years, were in the front ranks of all the meetings."[7]

Reporters were hostile to Buch; they were put off by her militancy and her rhetorical fireworks. They referred to her as "that Bush [sic] woman," and accused her, among other things, of being a "Russian communist" and a "naive kid." To which she replied, "I am here working and fighting for the workers. . . . We are not animals and we won't work in such conditions. . . . I'm not a kid. I am thirty. We're supposed to be Russians. Do we look like Russians to you? I should say we are not!"[8]

Though unfriendly, reporters couldn't help but note that Buch was effective. covering one of her speeches to workers at a mill in Pineville, North Carolina, on April 8, one reporter noted, "the outstanding feature of today's activities was a wild harangue against the mill 'bosses' and newspapers, police, and state militia by Vera Bush [sic] of New York. . . . [It was a] 1 hour 15 minute speech. . . . The workers appeared to be considerably inflamed by the Bush woman's harangue."[9]

Unsympathetic to Vera Buch, reporters were much more favorable to some of the other women leaders in Gastonia, especially Amy Schechter and Sophie Melvin. Both seemed to be much more "feminine" than Buch, less confrontational and not so ferocious.

Amy Schechter had been born in England, and was the daughter of an Oxford professor. She had attended Barnard College in New York City. Older than Buch, Schechter was thirty-seven in 1929. She represented "Workers International Relief" in Gastonia, a communist-inspired welfare organization. Years later Buch would write of Schechter:

On first impression she appeared odd. Although her thin aquiline face showed strength, she was somewhat sloppy, her clothes askew; her reddish-brown hair wound up in a knot in back looked uncombed. Her speech had a slight English accent, she talked fast and incoherently; she had some nervous twitchings of the face and shoulder. From her uncertainty it didn't look as though she had experience of this kind of work. . . . Eventually, when I got to know Schechter well, I valued her highly. She had guts. . . . Her little personal peculiarities didn't matter, though, for the strikers the first impression wasn't too good. As they couldn't pronounce her name, they referred to her as "that woman." But Amy worked hard, and her inborn kindliness and her dedication won their confidence.[10]

Schechter seemed "sophisticated" to people who met her. Mrs. Tom Hanna, wife of Gastonia's jailor, met Schechter when she was in jail, and Mrs. Hanna told reporters that Schechter "has a cultured voice, you should just hear her sing."[11] In the Gastonia strike Schechter had the unenviable job of trying to supply food and other supplies to the strikers. "I learned," Buch wrote, "to appreciate her reasonableness, her courage, her humor and wit, her cheerfulness. Amy was a good sport. Ask her to get up at three in the morning and walk five miles — if it was for the good of the union or Party, she would do it."[12]

Ellen Dawson was another prominent Gastonia strike leader.

Born in Scotland, Dawson had emigrated to the United States (without losing her Scots brogue), had found work in a mill, and had quickly joined a mill workers' union. She rushed South in 1929 to aid in the Gastonia struggle, and quickly became an indefatigable speaker. *Charlotte Observer* reporter Cora Harris recounted one of Dawson's speeches. Dawson "urged the women to step out and do their bit for there are 60 per cent women in the textile industry." "Resort to no violence," she warned them. "Come out and strike and stay on strike and everyone remain solid and we'll have 100% victory!" Dawson sat down and then a well-dressed and fiery young woman jumped to the platform and said: "Yes, they put me in jail, and I'm proud of it. I never done nothing to go to jail fer. They said it was fer disorderly conduct. Well I thank God I can stand up fer my rights and I'll go again and shed blood if it will keep this 'ere union!" Dawson and the crowd, Harris reported, roared their approval.[13]

The media's darling in Gastonia was Sophie Melvin.

Melvin too was a New Yorker, but in 1929 she was only nineteen and looked even younger. Vera Buch described her as "a remarkably pretty girl of nineteen years, sturdy, cheerful, and cooperative."[14] She was an activist in the Young Communist League and in Gastonia, her job was teaching and caring for the strikers' children. In the summer of 1929, when Sophie Melvin and the other leaders of the Gastonia strike were on trial for their live, court reporters couldn't restrain themselves from commenting on Melvin's youthful beauty. When the women defendants first entered the courtroom, for example, one reporter wrote as if they were in fashion show:

> Led by Amy Schechter, wearing a blue figured dress with her hair combed softly over the ears, they stepped into the courtroom smiling gaily and waving at friends among the textile workers who filled every available seat and stood near the doors. Vera Buck [sic] in a sleeveless green washable silk followed Amy, while Sophie Melvin, 19-year old brunette, came last, wearing a powder blue dress that set off perfectly the natural beauty for which she was praised by so many of the people in the courtroom.[15]

When Melvin stood to be arraigned, a "restrained gasp" could be heard among the trial spectators. Her "light blue frock" and "chestnut bobbed hair" immediately "set her off as the most attractive of the feminine contingent under arraignment. Some spectators whispered: 'Why isn't she pretty. . . . No jury will send that pretty girl to the electric chair.'"[16]

Gastonia, in fact, was crowded with women activists. Some were outsiders, who had come down to support the strike from up north, and others were local women workers who rallied to the strike cause.

Ella May Wiggins was one of the local women. She was a millhand from Bessemer City, where she worked at the American Mill. By 1929 Wiggins had lived what for many mill women was an archetypical life. Born in the mountains, she had married young and given birth to ten children in as many years. Her husband, John, "took off" and penniless, uneducated, and unskilled, Wiggins went into the mills. By the time she was thirty she was gaunt and weary. But when the strikes broke out, she rushed to join the movement. Wiggins, Vera Buch recalled, was "a short, sturdy woman of about thirty, with broad cheekbones, clear hazel eyes, and bobbed light brown hair. She had the deep-toned, chesty voice often heard in Slavic women. When I asked Ella May about her family origin, sure enough, that was it."[17] Buch continues:

> The woman who impressed me most was Ella Mae [sic] Wiggins. . . . She would write little ballads about the strike, set them to some well-known ballad tune, and sing them from the platform in a rich alto voice. Her rather gaunt face would light up and soften as she sang; her hazel eyes would shine; she became for the moment beautiful. She would often speak too, urging the strikers to remain firm. She appeared to be a person of unusual intelligence who grasped every feature of the strike and could explain it in her own words.[18]

Wiggins became one of the NTWU organizers in Bessemer City and even attempted to recruit African Americans into the union. By the late summer of the strike, she was one of the more prominent leaders of the movement.[19]

She would tell reporters that her chief concern was her children. Of her ten babies, five had died in infancy or childhood. "I was working nights and nobody to do for them," she said. "I asked the 'super' to put me on day shift so's I could tend 'em, but he wouldn't. . . . I don't know why. So I had to quit my job and then there wasn't any money for medicine, so they just died. I never could do anything for my children, not even to keep 'em alive, it seems. That's why I'm for the union, so's I can do better for them."[20]

Wiggins was shot to death by vigilantes on September 14, 1929.

It was, in a sense, no real surprise that women would be so actively involved in the strikes. Textile work was distinctly gendered. In 1850 some 64 percent of millhands in the textile industry were women; in 1900 women still made up some 50 percent of the workforce.[21] By 1930, in the South, men over age sixteen made up some 57.7 percent of the mill workforce; women over sixteen made up 38.5 percent of the workforce (and 3.8 percent of workers in the South were children under 16). Of women workers in the South in 1930, 44 percent were single, 45.2 percent were married, and the remaining 10.8 percent were divorced, separated, or widowed.[22]

Textile work had never paid very well, and in the 1920s, with the stretch-out, downward pressure on wages was intense. In 1920, for example, the average weekly wage for all manufacturing in the United States was around $33.81; the average weekly wage in cotton manufacturing was $24.86. By 1926 the average weekly wage in manufacturing had drifted down to around $32.54; in cotton manufacturing it was $17.48, which meant textile workers now made around 54 percent of the average manufacturing wage.[23]

Textile wages were low in general, particularly low in the South, and especially low for women. In Elizabethton, for example, the Glanzstoff plant employed 1,953 people in 1929. Of these, 1099 were men (56 %) and 854 (44 %) were women. They were paid as follows:

Selected Weekly Wage Rates at Glanzstoff
(percentage earning at specified rate)

Weekly Wage	% of all employees	% of men	% of women
$9-11.99	47	19.2	87.3
$12-14.99	30	48	8
$15-17.99	6.5	9.3	3.3

At the Bemberg plant a total of 958 employees, or 48 percent of the workforce, earned the lowest weekly wages: $9–$11.99. Of these 958 lowest paid employees, 746, or 78 percent, were women. On the other hand, there were 130 employees (6.5 % of the total workforce) who earned more than $26.00 each week; of these 130, 129 were men and one was a woman.[24] Little wonder then that women like Margaret Bowen were angry.

In the mills supposedly the more dangerous jobs went to men, the less dangerous jobs to women. Not only were the mills just as hot, just as lint-filled for women as for men, however, but the machines women ran were just as hazardous as those the men ran. The great roaring machines would catch you; they tore off fingers and broke bones. "Oh," millhand Alice Evitt remembered, "I've got my apron tore off of me in the speeder room. . . . I'd get my apron tore off of me two or three times a week. They'd wind me up, and I was just lucky I managed to stop 'em and didn't get my arms in them. Them fliers would break your bones. . . . I know one lady . . . she said . . . she'd [got] her hair caught and it pulled her whole scalp out — every bit of her hair."[25]

Another worker, Betty Davidson, remembered, "You always had to keep your hair close, and we wore dresses then, and I've had mine, just big chunks pulled out of them. And if you weren't careful, if you got caught in them, you know, it'd just jerk it off you."[26]

Women workers were central to the South's textile industry, and women workers took a prominent part in the strikes. The fact, then, that women were prominent in the press is evidence that reporters got the story right. It's not just that lots of women struck, however. As Jacquelyn Dowd Hall has written, women strikers, such as those in Elizabethton, were "unruly women." They were young, flamboyant, confrontational, and outrageous, southern versions of the Roaring Twenties' "New Woman."[27]

In a late April story, the *Elizabethton Star* reported that Bemberg-Glanzstoff officials had announced that the corporation would bring legal action against "women agitators and trespassers" who had, they charged, triggered the walkouts. According to the plant announcement, reported in the *Star*, "some of the most flagrant and brazen depredations were committed by women," who had entered the plants and had "cursed officials and otherwise insulted, abused and in certain instances attacked those who were engaged in the performance of their duties." The corporation had the names of some of these women and intended to swear out warrants for their arrest.[28] The *Star* added that in the strike parades, "many of the girls at the front of the parade were dressed in . . . men's trousers and several had flags and bunting draped around them."[29]

The *Charlotte News* reported a violent clash between strikers and scabs in Elizabethton in May. Scab cars, the *News* reported, tried to crash through the picket lines. Meanwhile, there were constant clashes between strikers and deputies. In one incident a "girl striker" and two male companions wrestled a pistol away from a deputy. Two National Guardsmen then jumped the girl and wrestled the gun away from her. Meantime, yet another "girl striker" was nearly killed when she leapt in front of a scab's car to prevent it from breaking the picket line.[30]

Cora Harris, reporting for the *Charlotte Observer*, wrote a story about a clash between some women strikers and the authorities in Gastonia:

> Women were the most outspoken and determined. One young woman of strong frame gave three or four policemen a first-class tussle before they landed her in a police car after arresting her for breaking through the militia's line in front of the mill's employment office and pummeling one of the guardsmen with a stout stick. . . . She told the guardsmen that a little thing like a bayonet wouldn't stop her and it didn't.

As the police drove her away, the crowd cheered her. "If Gastonia never realized that militant women were within its bounds, it certainly knows it now," Harris concluded.[31]

These unruly women had been molded by many of the same forces that had shaped the rest of the country. The Great War was one such force. Writing about the South for the *New York Times* in 1930, Anne O'Hare McCormick visited some of the old World War I training camps, and wrote:

> Go to any Southern town near a training camp and see what has happened to it since young men from all parts of the country mingled here. The merchants will tell you that "since the war" there is demand for a kind and variety of goods they never carried before. The preachers will tell you that their flocks are diminished and more worldly-minded. The planters and manufacturers will say that the working population is restless and independent, the labor turnover doubled or tripled.[32]

What the Great War didn't do, the popular culture of the Roaring Twenties did. Even in the poorest mill villages there were people with radios and cars, people who had been to movies or even been to Atlanta or Nashville. Young women in the most remote mill villages bobbed their hair, smoked cigarettes, and wore, on their Saturday afternoon after-work forays into town, their best imitation of big city fashion. Young men slicked their hair like Valentino and drank bootleg liquor. Huddled around their radios, southern millhands could hear, through the static, voices from New York City and Chicago. Millhands were, in fact, a modern industrial working class, not some ur-volk just emerging from the soil. Social worker Harriot Herring had spent a lifetime working in the mill villages, and she was sure that the young millhands of the 1920s were different. And, she added, mill managers hadn't a clue about how to deal with them. Managers still thought mill workers were starving farmers who would be eager to work docilely for sweat wages. They were wrong. In fact, Herring thought, "the public in general is likewise unaware of the new situation and the new worker."[33]

Not all the women in the newspaper stories were unruly. Anna Weinstock's role in the drama was quite different but to reporters just as fascinating. On May 8 a slightly built young woman arrived in Johnson City, Tennessee, near Elizabethton, and registered at the John Sevier Hotel. She signed in as "Anna Seidel." She immediately called on the pastor of St. Mary's church who knew Dr. Mothwurf, the Bemberg-Glanzstoff manager. She explained that her real name was Anna Weinstock, that she was from the Labor Department in Washington, and that she had been sent south to try to settle the strike. The pastor introduced her to Mothwurf.

Anna Weinstock was an unusual person. Born in Boston, she quit school as a teenager to get a job to support her family after her father died. She worked in a factory, quickly got elected an officer in her union local, became an active suffragist, and, not yet twenty-five, was elected president of the Massachusetts Women's Trade

Union League. In 1922 she was hired by the U.S. Department of Labor to work in its mediation service.

Weinstock played a key role in the grueling negotiations involved in working out a settlement in early May in Elizabethton. She tried to be an honest, behind-the-scenes broker, and concluded one dispatch to her boss in Washington with the note: "P.S. I am glad to be able to tell you that I have successfully escaped the notice of the press."[34]

She hadn't. In June 1929 stories about Weinstock appeared in papers throughout the country. The *Literary Digest*, a national magazine, published a profile of her. It began: "Settled by a woman! This is the fact that astounds the American newspaper editors." The profile makes Weinstock sound more like a Hollywood celebrity than a labor department civil servant. Weinstock was, the *Digest* explained, a "debonair" and "pretty 28-year old." Citing Associated Press reports, the Digest noted that Miss Weinstock had gone down to east Tennessee, to live "among some of the fightin'est of our pioneer stock" and had almost single-handedly ended the conflict.[35]

For a moment she became a minor celebrity. The *Charlotte Observer* wrote about her in a feature article called "Girl Who Played Big Part in Settlement of Rayon Mill Strike Finds Thrill in Job." The story gave something of Weinstock's background: "in the seven years of her experience as federal commissioner of conciliation she has heard — and tried to adjust, generally succeeding — the troubles of striking garment workers, textile workers, barbers, bakers, taxicab drivers, electricians, show workers, telephone operators, bricklayers, carpenters, and a dozen or more other kinds of workers."[36]

Her appearance was every bit as interesting to the story as her career. She "looked like a kid," the story explained,

> and was in fact only twenty-eight. Five feet five inches and 120 pounds of femininity: clean cut, even features, thick hair of dark brown that has never been bobbed, a penchant for blue — they call her here "the girl in blue"— pearly, even teeth, flashing brown eyes that look with level frankness into your own; a girl with a city air, yet quiet, businesslike and always to the point.[37]

Remarkable women were in the papers because they were in the strikes. They were also in the papers because the papers had been looking for flamboyant women all along.

In a matter of just a few weeks in the fall of 1930, for example, the *Danville Register* ran a series of vignettes, complete with photographs, about bold and racy women. On its front page the *Register* featured Mrs. Victor Bruce and her dog, Paddy, who attempted to fly from London to Tokyo; the "diminutive Australian aviatrix," Mrs. Keith Miller, who attempted to fly from New York City to Los Angeles; Miss Evelyn Jahncke, New Orleans' "most popular debutante," who suffered a nervous breakdown caused by "over study;" the alleged killer of Mary Baker, a "pretty young Navy Department clerk in Washington, D. C.," who was apprehended in Schenectady, New York; Miss Elizabeth Kelly, a twenty-one-year-old stenographer from Cleveland, who sued a millionaire for $100,000, claiming that they were engaged but that he jilted her (the *Register* reported that the millionaire insisted his relationship with Miss Kelly was strictly "confined to a series of parties"); and Miss Irma Loucks, of Portland, Oregon, who was charged with fatally stabbing the wife of her alleged lover.[38]

Consider the *Elizabethton Star*. Elizabethton, Tennessee, perched high up in the mountains, was about as far as you could get from anywhere and still be in the U.S.A. Yet the *Star*, by the late 1920s, was directly wired to the world's news. On the editorial page the *Star* included regular advice on investments in national business, a chit-chat column devoted to New York City gossip, and regular reports giving the "inside story" on Washington politics.[39] The paper's radio guide listed stations from New York City, Pittsburgh, Atlanta, Charlotte, Nashville, Richmond, Wheeling, Chicago, Cincinnati, Cleveland, and Detroit, all of which citizens of Elizabethton could pick up with their new radios.

Virtually every front page of the *Star* in 1929 featured a story about some world celebrity, typically a young woman, someone like movie star Alma Rubens (who denied having "peek-a-boo" adventures in Hollywood); or Rosita and Vivia Duncan (better known as "Topsy and Eva"), the famous dancers, who were returning from France; or Gilda Gray, the "shimmy queen" (who was getting a divorce).[40]

The *Star* was fascinated by the Twenties' "New Woman." In January 1929 she was present not just in the front-page stories about Hollywood stars. Human interest stories often featured independent-minded, assertive young women, like the "girls" with bobbed hair who worked for a telephone company in California, who rushed around the office on roller skates (the story was called "They Roll Along At Work);" or Elinor Smith, the "flying flapper," who piloted a plane for thirteen straight hours.[41] Young, daring, dangerous women grinned out from issue after issue. One photo showed seventeen-year-old Sylvia Szam of New York, with burly police officers on either arm; the caption explained "Girl Held as Gang Brains." The same issue included a picture of celebrity Ellen Wenzel dancing at a costume ball in Greenwich Village. A later issue included on the front page a photograph of tennis star Helen Wills with her fiance, the caption below explaining: "She Plays Love Set Now."[42] The *Star*'s comic page, meanwhile, included Bernard Dibble's cartoon character, "Danny," a Betty-Boop-style flapper, as well as the "Antics of Arabella," which consisted of photographs of young women in bathing suits doing exercises and swapping jokes ("These Girls Teach You Physical Culture While They Amuse You!" the caption promised). The *Star* was an enthusiastic supporter of the local high school girls' basketball team, the "Betsy Flashers."[43] The *Star* often serialized what it thought were the hottest new novels, and in January 1929 it ran one called "Confessions of a Gangster Girl," which was followed by "Ruby Worth – Bandit Girl."[44]

For some observers, however, Ruby Worth – Bandit Girl and her sisters on the picket lines were profoundly disturbing figures, and the reporting on the strikes echoes this sense of deep unease.

Some southern papers, the *Gastonia Daily Gazette* and the *Charlotte Observer*, for example, had already decided the central issue in the strikes was not economic justice but law and order.[45] Anarchy threatened to overwhelm law. Borders were constantly in danger of transgression. All these unruly women, fascinating as they might be, were also terrifying. They were the ones who constantly threatened to transgress one of the most emotionally charged of all frontiers, that of gender.

The mill strikes occurred within a specific historical and institutional context. This context was the peculiar mix of company town and intrusive, authoritarian, and ostensibly benevolent management known as "mill village paternalism." There is no shortage of theories about the origins and functions of mill village paternalism. But wherever it came from, it was linked both metaphorically and explicitly to masculine order. "Paternalism," historian Allen Tullos writes, "or fatherly authority, ranging from the despotic to the well intended, in relations both familial and societal, constituted a deep legitimizing force within white Piedmont society from the time of backwoods settlement through the era of capitalist industrialization." "To a child," Tullos observes, "religion, stoic discipline, fatherly authority, and the mill hierarchy seemed to be cut from the same cloth."[46] A mill superintendent "was just like the father of the whole shebang," one millhand told Tullos.[47] Mill owners liked to say that this masculine hierarchy was really the best sort of community. Everyone in the mill village was part of one "family," and the family was, of course, led by a powerful man.[48]

Whether this system was a carryover from slavery, as W. J. Cash thought; or a form of male control originally constructed for "unfortunate women," as Gary Freeze writes; or a way to impose bourgeois order on the unruly cracker proletariat, as David Carleton thinks; or a kind of social contract, as Douglas Flamming argues, mill village paternalism as a form of hierarchy and domination was clearly and directly besieged by the strikes.[49]

All these unruly women represented not only "lawlessness" in general, but a specific kind of gendered lawlessness known by nervous reporters as "free-lovism." Again and again newspapers reported outraged condemnations of the "free-lovism" allegedly propagated by trade-unionists, Reds, and outsiders. And althought presumably "free-lovism" involved both men and women, the strikes' opponents associated it especially with unruly and outrageous women.

North Carolina's Senator Overman worried deeply about "free-lovism" in his state. In defending mill owners from outside criticism, Overman insisted the strikes had been concocted by outside agitators, "communists," who sowed "the seeds of revolution, atheism, and free-lovism."[50] *The Southern Textile Bulletin*'s editor, David Clark, insisted that the "doctrine of free love, no religion, and social equality with negroes" were central communist beliefs. The Gastonia strike, Clark asserted, was provoked by assorted "radicals" and "communists," all connected to the Wobblies; "they profess to believe that Russia, with its socialism, social equality, free love, and atheism, is a heaven into which all workers should enter."[51] The *Charlotte Observer* reported Clark's comments in a page-one story. One *Observer* story, which reported that Gastonia strike leaders had encouraged women strikers to seduce National Guardsmen, was just one more bit of evidence that seemed to corroborate Clark's thesis.[52]

One of the virulent full-page ads in the *Gastonia Daily Gazette* warned grimly that what was at stake in the Gastonia strike was, among everything else, the "sanctity of marriage." The ad's radical bifurcation reflected the structure of the great dread that haunted the anti-union ranks. Law and order, patriotism, religion, property, and sexual discipline were all on one side; mob rule, violence, foreignness, atheism, attacks on property, and sexual anarchy were on the other. The former was clearly the "human" camp; the latter was the "alien" camp, which was, in its "seething hideousness," ready "to kill, ready to destroy property."[53] In one of its front-page editorials, the *Gazette* explained that communist doctrine "scoffs at all religion, believes in free-love, common ownership of property, and the domination of society through the instrumentality of the sword, [and] is so utterly un-American that it is inconceivable that it can gain a real foothold in the United States,"[54] though that, of course, was precisely the *Gazette*'s great fear.

Sexual anarchy was one of the recurring themes in the reporting on the trial of the Gastonia Seven, which took place in Charlotte in the summer of 1929. The prosecution called witnesses who told the jury, in hushed tones, all about the "goings-on" at union headquarters, all the "cursing and hugging and kissing."[55] The prosecution aggressively went after young Edith Miller, the wife of defendant Clarence Miller. Prosecutors demanded to know more about the Millers' personal life, about how long they had lived together, about whether they were legally married. Lead prosecutor John Carpenter demanded the defendants' conviction not only because of their alleged conspiracy to murder Gastonia's Police Chief Aderholt, but also because of their "debauchery."[56]

"Girls" were everywhere in the reporting on the textile wars. They were there because they were in the strikes; they were there too because reporters' eyes had been trained to see them. Fascinating and terrifying, all these "girls" created a peculiar hermeneutic. Stories about unruly women appeared in the press because unruly women appeared in the streets. Unruly women became visible in the streets, however, in part because they had first become visible in the magic mirror of the press.

All this brooding about gender and sexuality could take reporters in odd directions. For example, in the fall of 1930, on the eve of the Danville strike, the *Danville Register* published a curiously Freudian editorial about lynching. The *Register* was deeply disturbed by the increase in the number of lynchings from 1929 to 1930. The *Register* described lynchings as a "species of barbarism and anarchy." Why do these outrages occur? The *Register* doubted that economic hardship was to blame. Invariably, the *Register* argued, lynchings in the South occur in connection with real or alleged sexual crimes. The lynching itself, the paper insisted, is itself a kind of sexual crime. Lynching, the *Register* thought, was "nothing more than a group manifestation of the sexual crime of sadism." To be sure, the *Register* wasn't quite sure where to take this argument; it hoped, rather lamely, that someday science might explain it all. Of this the *Register* was sure, however, social disorder, vigilante violence, and sexual anarchy were all somehow connected to the inescapable question of race.[57]

NOTES

1. Anderson, "Elizabethton," *The Nation*, May 1, 1929, 527.

2. See Noel Sargent, "East Tennessee's Rayon Strikes of 1929," American Industries, June 1929, in Federal Mediation Service, NA RG 280-170-4869. Sargent offers a vigorous defense of management, and an equally vociferous attack on labor. Regarding employees, Sargent provides the following figures:

	Men	Women	Total	% women
Bemberg	886	384	1270	30
Glanzstoff	1099	854	1953	44
	1985	1238	3223	38

3. Anderson, "Elizabethton," *The Nation*, May 1, 1929, 526.

4. "Gaston . . . ," *CO*, April 2, 1929, 1.

5. "Many Favoring Early accord," *CO*, April 4, 1929, 3.

6. "Agitators Appeal to Women in Spurring Gastonia Strike," *CO*, April 5, 1929, 14. David Montgomery, writing about workers in the 1850s, notes:

> when urban workers organized their own parades they no longer appeared in their work garb, even when they were grouped by trade unions, but in street clothes, increasingly difficult to distinguish in style from those of he middle classes. Public processions of artisans Dressed for and performing their work, which had been characteristic of the late eighteenth-century civic pageantry, had been reduced by the 1830s to employers' advertisements of their wares. Workers celebrating or demanding their rights were attired as citizens.

See David Montgomery, *Citizen Worker* (New York: Cambridge University Press, 1993), 23.

7. Buch, *Life*, 212.

8. "Loray Strike Become Grim Waiting Game," *CO*, April 7, 1929, 1.

9. "Few On Jobs During Night at Pineville," *CO*, April 9, 1929, 13.

10. Buch, *Life*, 181.

11. "Women Prisoners Smile Gaily as They Enter Bitter Fight," *CO*, July 30, 1929, 10.

12. Buch, *Life*, 212.

13. "Agitators Appeal to Women in Spurring Gastonia Strike," *CO*, April 5, 1929, 14; "Woman Agitator Spurs Strike," *CO*, April 7, 1929, 2.

14. Buch, *Life*, 212.

15. "Women Prisoners Smile Gaily as They Enter Bitter Fight," *CO*, July 30, 1929, 10.

16. "Trial personalities," *CO*, July 30, 1929, 10.

17. Buch, *Life*, 218.

18. Buch, *Life*, 185.

19. Buch, *Life*, 208–9.

20. Margaret Larkin, "Ella Mae's Songs," *Nation*, October 9, 1929; also National Organization of Women, Charlotte-Metrolina Chapter, *Let's Stand Together: The Story of Ella Mae Wiggins* (Charlotte: National Organization of Women, 1979).

21. Herbert J. Lahne, *The Cotton Mill Worker* (New York: Farrar and Reinhart, 1944), 102.

22. Lahne, *Worker*, 290.

23. Lahne, *Worker*, 293; see discussion of wages, above, in Chapter 3.

24. Data taken from U.S. Senate, Committee on manufactures, 71st Congress, May 8, 9, and 20, 1929, 97. See also: Tippett, *Labor*, 56. Sargent, in "East Tennessee's Rayon strikes," takes exception to union claims of low wages. Even Sargent's calculations indicated, however, that wages were indeed on the low side. Weekly wages according to Sargent were as follows:

	Glanzstoff		Bemberg	
Amount	Men	Women	Men	Women
$9–11.99	212	746	14	86
12–14.99	530	69	38	200
15–17.99	102	28	95	107
18–20.99	74	5	301	39
21–25.99	51	5	94	7
26–28.99	32	0	106	8
29–31.99	21	0	38	2
32–34.99	12	0	38	1
35–40.99	43	1	35	2
41–42.99	15	0	35	0
50.00+	7	0	17	0
	1099	854	811	452

25. Evitt Interview, UNC-CH, SOHP.

26. Davidson Interview. UNC-CH, SOHP.

27. Hall, "Women," 373.

28. "Sen. Wheeler urges Probe be conducted," *ES*, April 29, 1929, 1.

29. "Kelly Appeals to Head of Federation," *ES*, May 8, 1929, 1.

30. "Grave Trouble Threatens After Dynamiting in Elizabethton Area," *CN*, May 16, 1929, 1.

31. "Women Take Active Part in Gastonia Mill Strike," *CO*, April 4, 1929, 3.

32. Anne O'Hare McCormick, "The South: Its Second Reconstruction," *NYT*, June 8, 1930, V, 4.

33. Herring, "Present Textile Industry," in Herring Papers, SHC, UNC-CH.

34. Letter from Anna Weinstock to Hugh Kerwin, May 13, 1929, Labor Conciliation Service, NA RG 280 170-4869.

35. "Rays of Sunshine in the Rayon War," *Literary Digest*, June 8, 1929, 12.

36. "Girl Who Played . . . ," *CO*, June 2, 1929, III, 1.

37. "Girl Who Played Big Part in Settlement of Rayon Mill Strike Finds Thrill in Job," *CO*, June 2, 1929, III, 1.

38. "On Long Air Trip," DR, October 4, 1930, 1; "Seeks Continental Flight Record," *DR*,

October 10, 1930, 1; "Too Much Study, Deb Collapses," *DR*, November 15, 1930, 1; "Say He Admitted Murder of Girl," *DR*, November 18, 1930, 1; "Asks $100,000 In Love Suit," *DR*, November 20, 1930, 1; "Girl Held on Murder Charge," *DR*, November 25, 1930, 1.

39. The *Star*'s columns included "Washington Daily Comment," by John Nevin; the "Investment Bureau" (unsigned), and "New York by Day and Night," by Louis Sobel.

40. "Peek-a-boo Denied by Alma," *ES*, January 10, 1929, 1; "Rosita and Vivian Return," *ES*, January 12, 1929, 1; "Shakes Hubby for Good," *ES*, January 18, 1929, 1; "Babe Ruth Grieves Tragic Death of Wife," *ES*, January 14, 1929, 1.

41. "They Roll Along at Work," *ES*, January 16, 1929, 1; "Girl Flyer Sets Record," *ES*, January 31, 1929, 1.

42. "Girl Held as Gang Brains," *ES*, and "Dances at Ball," *ES*, January 22, 1929, 1; "She Plays Love Set Now," *ES*, January 26, 1929, 1.

43. "Meet the Betsy Flashers" (editorial), *ES*, January 18, 1929, 4.

44. Both serialized novels ran in January 1929. The *Star* does not identify the authors.

45. See, for example: "The First Breach of Faith" (editorial), *CO*, April 24, 1929, 8; also, "Leaders jailed as Strikers Attempt Third Parade at Loray," *CO*, April 25, 1929, 1.

46. Tullos, *Habits*, 77; 10.

47. Tullos, *Habits*, 11.

48. Cited in McLaurin, *Paternalism*, 47–8.

49. All of the literature on the textile industry addresses the issue of "paternalism." For an introduction to this issue, see, for example: Gary R. Freeze, "Poor Girls . . . ," in Leiter et al., *Thread*; McLaurin, *Paternalism*, especially Chapter 3, "The Mind of Owner and Operative;" Tullos, *Habits*, 8–11; 178–80, and elsewhere; Hall et al., *Family*, Chapter 3; Flamming, *Creating*, 121, 360.

50. "Farmers Dominate Gastonia Trial Jury," *NYT*, October 4, 1929, 19.

51. David Clark, "Communism," *STB*, September 19, 1929, 17. Also: "Clark Scouts Importance of Youth's Strike at Gastonia: Publisher declares Communistic Program of Free Love and Inter-Racial Intercourse Misses Fire," *CO*, April 6, 1929, 1.

52. "Agitators Appeal to Women in Spurring Gastonia Strike," *CO*, April 5, 1929, 14; "Strikers . . . Ask Women to Urge Soldiers to Refuse Duty," *CN*, April 9, 1929, 4.

53. "Mob Rule vs. Law and Order," *GDG*, April 4, 129, 7.

54. "Time for Sober Thought" (editorial), *GDG*, April 5, 1929, 1.

55. "Eye Witnesses Tell of Aderholt Killing," *CO*, September 6, 1929, 12; "'Shoot to Kill!' Witness Quotes Beal," *CO*, September 8, 1929, 1.

56. "Where Oratory Still Witches" (editorial), *NYT*, October 21, 1929, 26.

57. "Social Diagnosis of Lynching," *DR*, September 29, 1930, 4

6

The Inescapable Question of Race

In May 1929 the *Charlotte News* reported North Carolina Governor O. Max Gardner's speech to the State Inter-Racial Conference in Raleigh. The Governor spoke enthusiastically and optimistically about race relations in North Carolina; they were, he thought, "remarkable." "There is nothing more interesting to me," he said, "than the sociological study of the American white and colored man living together, side by side, especially in the South, on terms of friendship and good will. In spite of an occasional and fanatical injustice done, I am convinced that the finest evidence of the white man's conception of justice and fair play is found in his attitude to the negro."[1] "Race relations in North Carolina," the *Raleigh News and Observer* happily reported, "have reached the point where the chief complaint registered at the annual meeting of the State Inter-Racial Commission here yesterday was that "things are too quiet for keeping up interest in local race commissions."[2]

Outrages still occurred, of course. In July 1930 in Wilson County, North Carolina, a twenty-nine-year-old African-American tenant farmer named Oliver Moore was accused by his white landlord of attacking the landlord's two small daughters. The girls ended up in the hospital. Moore tried to flee but was caught and taken across the county line and put in the Edgecombe County jail. In the dark of night on August 18, a mob of some 200 masked men stormed the Edgecombe County jail, seized Moore, and dragged him back across the county line. According to reporters, "the mob carried him into Wilson County, a stone's throw from the spot where the crime was committed, strung him from a tree and shot him to death. Suspended by two plowlines passed under his arm pits, the Negro's body hung from a limb of a giant pine tree until 9 o'clock [the next morning]." The coroner's jury, called immediately to consider Moore's killing, "reached no verdict."[3]

Such ghastly rituals were, thankfully, becoming rare, at least in the upper South. Newspapers such as the *Richmond Times-Dispatch* bitterly denounced mob violence. The *Times-Dispatch* went even further, and attacked those "very decent folk" who would never join a mob themselves but who "murmur" that well, maybe such lynchings are justified as a kind of spontaneous people's justice. Perhaps, the *Times-Dispatch* admitted, when proper authorities are really unwilling or unable to act, citizens can take the law into their own hands. In general, it insisted, such mob actions are nothing more than savagery. Lynching reflects "not a desire to promote the ends of justice, but a base and cowardly desire to inflict pain and torture upon a defenseless person." Governor Gardner, when informed of the Moore lynching, was outraged and appalled and denounced it as "a disgrace to North Carolina." He vowed to use all his power to support the efforts of local authorities (which would be unsuccessful) to apprehend and punish the members of the mob. It was small comfort to know that Moore's lynching was the first ever in Wilson County, and the first in North Carolina since 1921.[4]

"In the 1920s," historian George Tindall writes, "the new peculiar institution of Negro subordination had reached its apogee as an established reality in law, politics, economics, and folkways. . . . The question was settled." In fact, though, as Tindall points out, the race question was far from settled.[5]

Race had, it would seem, nothing to do with the strike wave of 1929–31. Mill work was strictly segregated; it was "white man's work," and though a few African Americans worked in some mills, always in the lowest paying of low paying jobs, virtually the whole mill workforce, and of course all the mill owners, were white. Race, it would seem, had nothing to do with it.

In 1929, however, race, in the southern press, was as much an obsession as ever, and inevitably reporting on class became all tangled up with assumptions about race.

In the fall 1928 elections, the 1st Congressional district of Illinois, southside Chicago, sent Oscar DePriest to the U.S. Congress. When, early in 1929, Congressman DePriest was assigned an office in Washington, his neighbor, George Pritchard, a North Carolina Congressman, was enraged. Oscar DePriest was an African American, and Pritchard refused to have an office next to a black man. Pritchard's behavior became a public issue. Most southern papers rushed to his defense. The *Charlotte Observer*, for instance, insisted that "the people of the State will sympathize with Rep. Pritchard,"[6] and the *Raleigh News and Observer*, much more liberal than the *Charlotte Observer* on most issues, was positively livid about DePriest's election.[7]

The DePriest issue simply wouldn't go away. When the First Lady invited the wives of newly elected congressmen to the White House, she of course included Mrs. DePriest; the southern press was furious. DePriest's nomination of young African Americans to West Point and Annapolis ignited another explosion; the southern white press attacked DePriest, and the black press just as enthusiastically defended him.[8]

In a long editorial the *Raleigh News and Observer* argued that former North Carolina Governor Charles Aycock, "the best friend the Negro ever had in North Carolina," had offered the best counsel the paper had ever heard on race relations. Reacting to President Theodore Roosevelt's meeting in the White House with

Booker T. Washington, Aycock insisted that he and the white people of the South wanted only the best for black southerners. Speaking at the state fair in Raleigh in 1901, Governor Aycock told blacks that

> inside of your own race you can grow as large and broad and high as God permits, with the aid, the sympathy, and the encouragement of your white neighbors. If you can equal the white race in achievement . . . you will find no generous minded white man who will stand in your way; but all of them in the South will insist that you shall accomplish this high end without social intermingling. And this is well for you, it is well for us, it is necessary for the peace of our section.

Aycock then issued an ominous warning to black North Carolinians: "the law which separates you from the white people of the State socially always has been and always will be inexorable, and it need not concern you or me whether the law is violated elsewhere. It will never be violated in the South. Its violation would be to your destruction as well as to the injury of the whites." This, the *News and Observer* insisted, was the best counsel anyone could offer on the matter of race.[9]

The textile industry was a whites-only industry, but in fact, in the textile industry race had always been entangled with class. One of the biggest mill complexes in the South was the Riverside and Dan River company in Danville, Virginia. Danville, historically, was a tobacco town. Some of Danville's tobacco brokers had made small fortunes before the Civil War. After the war Danville had fewer than 8000 residents, of whom around half were African Americans. During slave days, of course, Danville's black residents had no say whatsoever in town affairs. After the end of slavery, however, during Reconstruction, Danville's black residents had formed a coalition with a handful of whites, and this coalition threatened to replace Danville's traditional tobacco-merchant elite. As long as Federal bayonets hedged about the coalition, Danville's old elite could only watch sullenly. After the end of Reconstruction in 1877, however, Danville's old elite planned its comeback. The black-white coalition won local elections in late 1882; blacks were appointed to public office and there were even black police officers. The next year, 1883, Danville exploded in a bitter race riot that left four blacks dead and propelled the town's old politicians back into power.

The old white elite was convinced that its return to power had to be part of a wider restructuring of Danville's society, and that a critical part of that restructuring was cementing the racial ties between rich and poor whites. According to Hattie Hylton, the superintendent of welfare at the Dan River Mills, this was all part of the context that inspired the creation of the mills. She explained, in a 1915 talk, that Danville in the 1880s was

> a struggling town, whose population was made up of as many negroes as there were white people, a condition which was at that time a great menace to the well-being of the community. The tobacco business gave to the negroes ample opportunity to make a living, while there was

nothing whatever to afford the least chance for the poor and illiterate white people. . . . Something must be done to relieve this unequal and galling situation.[10]

What was done, she went on, was the creation of the cotton mills. White solidarity was part of the bargain of paternalism; white owners would make sure that white workers always had a job, and the segregated nature of mill work was a tangible expression of this racial pact. The mills were cornerstones of the South's class and race architecture. Mill village paternalism would tie white labor to white capital by a thousand bonds of interest and affection; mill jobs would be white-only and guarantee work for whites and thus prevent any future coalition between white and black workers.

Race, then, was the key to defusing class. So long as white workers could be convinced that their racial bond with their white betters was stronger than any class differences that might divide them, the South's white upper classes could enjoy their privileges in tranquility.

Segregation, though, was not an unmixed blessing for capital. Wages in the mills in the late 1800s and early 1900s were far too low to attract even the poorest European immigrants, and if black southerners were automatically excluded from the mills, then white southerners would have something of a labor monopoly on mill work. When the textile business was good, and management needed more workers, management would have to turn to the South's native whites, who would have a distinct bargaining advantage. Some managers experimented with the idea of bringing blacks into the mills as even cheaper labor than poor whites, and thus driving down wages for everyone. White workers, not surprisingly, reacted furiously, and part of white worker racism was rooted in this fear that mill management would use cheap black labor to force wages down.[11]

The insular nature of the mill villages also contributed to white tribalism. People on the mill hills worked together, played together, worshiped together, and married each other. Far more than farmers, or city folk, or other industrial workers, millhands were perceived, and perceived themselves to be, a tribe apart. If all this togetherness fostered a strong sense of community identity and mutual help, it also generated that closed, clannish quality commentators so often noted about millhands.[12] For example, after the vigilante raid on union headquarters in Gastonia in April 1929, Governor Max Gardner secretly hired a private detective named Robert Lumsden, and sent him off to Gastonia to ferret out the vigilantes. Lumsden hurried off to Gastonia, checked in with state solicitor John Carpenter, and then spent some six weeks in and around Gastonia sniffing for clues. Lumsden did learn about one man who might know something, but he had disappeared off to Georgia. Another man, Lumsden reported back, was "literally scared to death" and wouldn't say anything. In the end, detective Lumsden learned nothing. In frustration, he reported to Governor Gardner, "it is an impossibility, it seems, to get anything worthwhile direct from any of these mill workers; either the 'ins' or the 'outs.' They are simply *NOT* going to talk to anyone."[13] Abandoning the investigation, Lumsden concluded, "if anybody outside of the raiding party knows anything about it they have kept consistently quiet on the subject and of course the raiders themselves are keeping quiet."[14]

Black southerners were outside this particular white tribe. True, some of the better-off millhands actually could afford to hire black "help" in the house, a cook or cleaning lady, and some of the poorest of the millhands lived in mixed-race rural villages, but most millhands, though not necessarily negrophobic, would have thought mixing with blacks utterly out of the question. As one millhand told Douglas Flamming, the very idea of a black family living in a mill village was "literally unspeakable."[15]

In Gastonia, it was the communists who first spoke the unspeakable, and amazingly enough, it was the respectable classes, not the millhands in particular, who were enraged. Reporting on the communists' calls for an end to segregation, for example, the *Charlotte News*, in an editorial, fiercely denounced the "sinister gospel of racial equality."[16]

Fred Beal had serious doubts about the tactical wisdom of raising the racial issue in the middle of the strike, but nevertheless, he spoke openly about it. The NTWU, he insisted, was all for racial equality. To the strikers, Beal insisted, "there must be no division between white and colored workers. We must take in every colored worker. We are not going to make them scabs. If he is good enough to work in the mill with you he is good enough to be in the union."[17]

The *Gastonia Daily Gazette* was beside itself. In a front-page editorial devoted to Beal and his fellow Reds, the *Gazette* insisted that "it is high time they were being deported from Gaston county. Get them out of here." The editorial continued,

> They advocate racial equality, inter-marriage of whites and blacks . . . etc., etc. Here is their platform:
> 1. A federal law against lynching.
> 2. Abolition of the whole system of race discrimination. Full . . . equality for the negro race.
> 3. Abolition of all Jim-Crow laws.
> 4. Abolition of all laws which disfranchise the negroes.
> 5. Abolition of laws forbidding intermarriage of persons of different races.
> 6. Abolition of all laws . . . which prohibit . . . negro children . . . from attending general public schools or universities.
> 7. Full and equal admittance of negroes to all railway station waiting rooms, trains, restaurants, hotels and theaters.
> How long are the authorities going to put up with this sort of drivel? How much longer will the good people of this community stand for stuff like this?[18]

The *Charlotte Observer* was just as horrified. In an editorial entitled "Will the Workers Stand for It?" the *Observer* remarked:

> Doubtless it was a surprise to some people in the Carolinas to learn a few days ago that the Communist strike leaders, Fred Erwin Beal and George Pershing, favored negroes being admitted to their union on a basis of entire equality with the whites, and it is doubtful if all

even yet realize that entire equality between the races is one of the cardinal aims of the Communists.[19]

In early May the *Observer* raised the issue of race again. After denouncing Beal, Weisbord, Pershing, and "others of the ilk" for duping workers, the *Observer* specifically denounced Weisbord's ideas about racial equality: "Weisbord boldly pleaded for the inclusion of the negro in the union." Some have dismissed accusations of racial fraternization, the *Observer* noted, as little more than anti-union propaganda, but Weisbord's own words prove that he and his allies seriously wanted racial equality.

Those who do not like the charge that the Loray strike was instituted and backed by Communists and that they advocate racial equality in the South should blame nobody but the promoters of the strike and the leaders of the strikers. But those who would mix the white textile workers of North Carolina with the negroes in unions or in any other organizations will find that it can not be done.[20]

A few weeks later, in another editorial, the *Observer* again shuddered at the idea of race-mixing. "And so the Communists are trying to get the negro janitors, domestic help, laundry workers, etc. into the union," the editorial began. It is inconceivable that white Carolinians would ever accept such a plan. The editorial concluded, "the day will come when Beal, Pershing, and . . . others . . . couldn't be hired to show their faces to those Loray workers who are now following their leadership."[21]

Race was central to the prosecution's strategy at the trial of the Gastonia Seven, and of course the press enthusiastically reported everything about the trial. Questioning union worker Dewey Martin, for example, assistant prosecutor E. T. Cansler demanded to know whether Martin had ever spoken on the same stage as Otto Hall, a "negro." Tom Jimison, for the defense, immediately objected. Judge Barnhill excluded the jury and demanded to know what the prosecution was up to. Cansler explained:

We propose to show that this witness spoke on the same platform with a negro named Otto Hall, on which social equality was advocated between the black and white races. . . . I am arguing that as part of the conspiracy in this case they were advocating and carrying on a movement not only for the purpose of inciting strikes in Gastonia but for the purpose . . . to organize colored helpers on the farms that they might cause riot in this country.

Jimison responded heatedly that the issue at hand was an accusation of second degree murder, not race-mixing. Well, "if teaching racial equality does not tend to impeach a witness," prosecutor Cansler angrily replied, "I do not know what would."

Prosecutor Jack Newell then interjected, "This union . . . is striving to array class against class for the specific purpose of overthrowing this government. Of course I know that is impossible, but the union is inciting strikers and bargaining with the negro workers on farms throughout the south so they can riot and overthrow the government."[22]

Judge Barnhill ruled for Jimison.[23] Later, when the prosecution doggedly brought the race issue up yet again, Barnhill, according to news reports, "agreed with Mr. Cansler that advocacy of race equality in the South, under the conditions prevailing in this region, was reprehensible, but that it would not be fair to bring this question before the jury."[24]

If the argument about class immediately inspired an argument about race, the reverse was true, too. For instance, the *Charlotte Observer* noted that a recent book had appeared entitled *What the Negro Thinks*. Well, the paper thought, negroes ought to know what white people think. "The white man," the editorial explained, "has little confidence in the negro as a race, because the negro has done and is doing nothing to merit that confidence. The negro wants without working for it all that the white man has attained through centuries of tribulation." To be sure, the editorial noted, a handful of negroes had accomplished something. There were negro teachers, scientists, and business people, and that was commendable. The problem, however, was that the vast majority of negroes were workers, and as workers they were pitiful. The editorial stated,

> It is here that the negro fails lamentably in measuring up to specifications. He is unstable and undependable and he must be continually watched to insure that he delivers a full day's work for a full day's pay. When the weather is fine and the going easy, he will not work at all. This is particularly true of domestic labor. Servants leave without notice, and as often as not they do not leave with empty hands.

The negro, the editorial concluded, "by his own acts has forced the white man to look upon him with suspicion and distrust." Until that changed, there could never be any white confidence in the negro, and it went without saying that "the negro of course can never expect to attain social equality in the South. Well-informed and sensible negroes realize that this is so, and are teaching their youth not to aspire to the impossible."[25]

(Throughout, of course, as in all southern papers, the word "negro" was insistently spelled with a lower-case "n." It would be some years before the press would promote the "n" to an upper-case.)

A few days later the *Observer* took up the theme again. Some deluded people claim, said the *Observer*, that a handful of noisy communists can't do any real harm, but that, the editorial retorted, favorably citing views expressed by the *Charleston News and Courier*, was absurd. A handful of communists can indeed do great damage, above all by inciting the negro; "the negro is the proletarian of this country, and it is organizing of the negroes that is the chief aim of the Communists — and here it might be well to suggest to the colored preachers that they put their flocks on guard." The communists' aim, the *Observer* continued, was to forge an alliance between "a few white working men" and "hordes of Southern negroes." On the one hand, the editorial insisted, such an alliance would be impossible, and yet the very act of agitation for it, the editorial concluded nervously, was a grave danger.[26] "Hordes," of course, was hardly a neutral term. Barbarians travel in "hordes," and the fact that "hordes" of "negroes" were loose in the South was, to much of the white press, a point of constant terror.

Nowhere was the link between race and class more incandescent than in the mind of David Clark, prominent Charlotte citizen, entrepreneur, journalist, and editor of the *Southern Textile Bulletin.*[27]

To Clark, the tie between unions, communists, subversion, free-lovism, and negro equality was entirely clear.

In an interview with the *Charlotte Observer*, Clark denounced the "communistic program of free love and inter-racial intercourse." The strike at Loray, as far as he could tell, attracted mostly "boys and girls," who, "being young . . . were easily led into disorders." What really infuriated him, though, was the NTWU's call for racial equality within the union: "their demand that negroes be admitted to the union on an equal basis with whites is in keeping with an editorial in their official organ, the *Daily Worker* . . . on March 29, 1929, which . . . insisted upon white girls dancing with negro men 'to break down capital-instilled prejudices.'"[28]

The *Southern Textile Bulletin*'s editorial page all through 1929 was filled with the most frantic warnings about an impending racial apocalypse. In mid-April the *Bulletin* quoted the *Daily Worker*'s call for white girls to dance with negro men, and asked shrilly, "can the mill operatives of the South, the purest blooded Anglo-Saxon people in the United States, afford to join an organization which demands that white girls dance with negro men?"[29]

The following week the *Bulletin* insisted that the vigilante attack on union headquarters in Gastonia was no surprise, since the union was led by communists "who are opposed to all religion, believe in free love, negro equality, and openly advocate the overthrow of our Government."[30] In July the *Bulletin* reprinted an editorial from the *Gastonia Gazette* that warned that communists advocated racial equality, and in another editorial mocked New Yorkers who attacked the South as racist but who had no use for blacks either. "The truth is," the *Bulletin* wrote, "that negroes who behave themself [sic], and do not seek social equality, are in less danger and are better treated in the South than in the North, but all the communists in the world cannot force the South or any group of Southern white men to accept the negro as their social equal."[31]

In August the *Bulletin* printed a photograph of two young boys setting off for Russia as part of a Communist Party delegation from the United States. One boy was black; the white boy was Elmer McDonald from Gastonia. The *Bulletin* was livid. It didn't blame young Elmer. "Someday," the *Bulletin* warned, however, Elmer's "Anglo-Saxon McDonald blood may assert itself, and he may refuse to sleep and live with negroes. Then he may arise and curse the parents who so lost their sense of decency as to consider their son as the social equal of negroes and low-class Russians.[32]

There was much more. Again and again the *Bulletin* denounced "social equality with negroes," and warned against inter-racial marriage.[33] It ascribed these "rotten" ideas to communists, but insisted that all trade-unionists endorsed them. On the issue of race, the *Bulletin* argued, the United Textile Workers were almost as radical as the communists. That was quite untrue, to be sure. If anything, the UTW went out of its way to be "sensitive" to white southerners' racial obsessions. That mattered little to the *Bulletin*.[34]

The 1929 strikes dramatized the link between race and class to black southerners, too, but the conclusions they drew were quite different from those of David Clark. The *Star of Zion* was the official weekly newspaper of the African Methodist Episcopal Zion Church. Founded in 1876, it was published in Charlotte and edited by Rev. W. H. Davenport. The *Star* was, like the church itself and Charlotte's black "better class,"[35] prudent, articulate, and circumspect. The *Star*'s articles included reports on bishops's conferences and laity conventions, clergy assignments and promotions, budgets and programs and innovations, and reviews of theological debates and exhortations for greater piety. The paper was, of course, deeply interested in African-American affairs, but otherwise, rarely mentioned other secular news. Coming from Charlotte, though, the *Star* could hardly avoid commenting on the chaos in the mills.

On the one hand, it would seem, race had nothing to do with the mill troubles; "color prejudice hardly entered the situation," the *Star* noted. The issue of "racial equality" was a red herring. The paper asserted that "to try to drag in the nightmare of social equality is unworthy of us. The Negro here wants work . . . with a liberal wage. He covets the rights of citizenship and the protection of the law. . . . He has, in no way, been involved in the strike. . . . What the Negro wishes is to be kept out of the tragedy."[36]

Yet, the *Star* argued, black southerners could not avoid entanglement with this fight among whites. For one thing, there was a curious parallel between the lot of blacks and that of poor whites:

> That injustice and intolerance are not always based on racial differences is demonstrated in the trial of some sixteen strike promoters who are charged with murdering the chief of police in the mill troubles. . . . The strike was due to the almost absolute serfdom in which the mill hands were kept by the Southern mill owners and from which they were striving to free themselves.[37]

The *Star* was, like most southerners black and white, shocked by the outburst of vigilante violence — shocked but not surprised. The vigilantes, the *Star* wrote,

> have learned these methods by their unpunished attacks on accused Negroes. What is systematically practiced against Negroes will be performed occasionally against white people — or against any people. . . . Lawlessness and crime do not discriminate. . . . It matters not that some of the strikers and some of their leaders were Communists. That had nothing to do with the right of self-defense or the crime of murder. . . . Colored people need to be

concerned about this trial of white people. . . . If whites who are poor and disadvantaged have no rights to self-defense and no rights to legal procedure, the blacks will know where they stand.[38]

The *Star of Zion* was a staid church paper, disinterested in most worldly matters. Yet the *Star*'s commentaries about the mill situation included an astonishingly radical conclusion:

They who produce the wealth of the world are entitled to its enjoyment. And the wealth of the nation should not be controlled by a small factional part of it. As long as it is so controlled and men and women are compelled to labor for a pauper's wage, there will be discontent, strikes, which neither threats nor violence, bayonets, nor bastilles can suppress. Well-fed, well-housed, and contented people neither strike, rob, nor steal. It is the haunting fear of misery which poverty entails — when hunger and want feed on their bosoms, and ill-gotten wealth, ground out of sweat and toil, flaunts its vanities and vices in the faces of its producers, that the deeps of discontent and resentment are stirred.[39]

The *Star*'s long concern with race had inspired its remarkable convictions about class. As polar opposites as the white millhands and black southerners were, the fact of oppression, the *Star* was convinced, had in an odd way made them, for a moment at least, in suffering and injustice, one.

NOTES

1. "Gardner Describes Inter-Racial Status in N.C. as 'Remarkable,' *CN*, May 8, 1929, 2.
2. "Social Equality Not Negro Goal, Moton Declares," *RNO*, May 8, 1929, 1.
3. "Gardner Will Seek To Punish Mob Members," *RT-D*, August 20, 1930, 1.
4. "Mob Violence" (editorial), *RTD*, August 23, 1930, 4; "Gardner Will Seek to Punish Mob members," *RTD*, August 20, 1930, 1. A month later, a similar horror occurred in Thomasville, Georgia. Willie Kirkland, a young trustee at the county jail, was accused of attacking a white girl. A mob seized Kirkland and three other black men and dragged them before the girl. She insisted that Kirkland had been her assailant. The mob then dragged Kirkland away, hanged him, and shot him repeatedly. The county Sheriff told the coroner's jury that he could not identify anyone in the mob. No one was every prosecuted for Kirkland's murder. See "Negro is Killed by Georgia Mob in Girl's Attack," *RTD*, September 26, 1930, 6; "The Lynching Crime," *RTD*, October 24, 1930, 12.
5. Tindall, *Emergence*, 160.
6. "The Least of the Trouble" (editorial), *CO*, April 8, 1929, 8.
7. "Pritchard To Be Furnished Other Office Quarters," *RNO*, April 8, 1929, 1; "Negro Congressman's Wife Attends White House Tea," *RNO*, June 14, 1929, 1; "DePriest Meets Social Waterloo at Musical Show," *RNO*, June 23, 1929, 1; "DePriest Affair Now Recalls Roosevelt-Washington Episode," *RNO*, June 23, 1929, 9; "Hoover and the DePriest Affair," *RNO*, June 30, 1929, 12; "Negro Flings Charges of Cowardice at the South," *RNO*, July 3, 1929, 1; "List of Negroes at White House," *RNO*, July 4, 1929, 1; "Political Effect of Inviting Negro Congressman's Wife to the White House Tea," from the *Lynchburg News*, *RNO*, July

4, 1929, 4; "Upholds Condemnation of Social Mingling of Races," *RNO*, July 6, 1929, 1; "Commission of Negro Revoked," *RNO*, July 11, 1929, 1.

8. For an example of the white press's reporting see, for instance, "Negro Congressman Is Proving Problem in Political Circles," *GDN*, April 9, 1929, 1; "Pritchard May Gain Strength as Result of D'Priest Incident," *GDN*, September 7, 1929, 1; "Pritchard Not To Be Near Chicago Negro, DePriest," *GDG*, April 11, 1929, 7; "Condemns Mrs. Hoover for Entertaining Negro Woman," *GDG*, June 15, 1929, 10. For a summary of the response of the African American press, see: "Color in Congress," *SofZ*, June 13, 1929, 2; "Mrs. DePriest at the White House (editorial)," *SofZ*, June 20, 1929, 4; "What's All the Shouting For?" *SofZ*, June 20, 1929, 1; "A Tea to Which A Negro Was Invited," *SofZ*, June 27, 1929, 1; "The Negro Press on the Hoover-DePriest Dinner," *SofZ*, July 4, 1929, 6; "Many Presidents Have Been Hosts to Negroes, Report," *SofZ*, July 11, 1929, 1. See also Tindall, *Emergence*, 252–53.

9. "Governor Aycock on Social Equality," *RNO*, June 26, 1929, 4.

10. Hattie E. Hylton, Superintendent of Welfare Work, Dan River Cotton Mills, "A Fifteen Minute Talk On The Schoolfield Welfare Work," given at the Welfare Conference of Southern Employers, Black Mountain, North Carolina, July 16, 1915, Danville Public Library, *Clippings*, indexed by Clara G. Fountain, Vol. 8, 158–65.

11. See Carlton, *Mill*, 244–45.

12. One of the great discoveries of recent studies of mill village life has been the millhands' intense sense of community, mutual aid, and cooperation; this is one of the central points of Hall et al.'s *Family*. Douglas Flamming points out the other side to this intense sense of community: "Historians have become so enamored with the idea of 'community' that they have often lost sight of its darker implications. The underside of community was coercion . . . [which] squelched individual freedom," Flamming, *Creating*, 165.

13. Letter from R. L. Lumsden to Governor O. Max Gardner, April 30, 1929, Gardner Papers, File 112, N.C. State Archives.

14. Letter from R. L. Lumsden to Governor O. Max Gardner, May 9, 1929, Gardner Papers, File 112, N. C. State Archives.

15. Flamming, *Creating*, 165.

16. "There Will Be Time For This" (editorial), *CN*, April 14, 1929, 8.

17. "Communists Threaten . . . ," *CO*, April 5, 1929, 1.

18. "If Leaders Were Gone," (editorial), *GDG*, April 12, 1929, 1.

19. "Will Workers Stand for It?" (editorial), *CO*, April 18, 1929, 8.

20. "It Can't Be Done" (editorial), *CO*, May 7, 1929, 8.

21. "Will They Accept Negroes?" (editorial), *CO*, May 14, 1929, 8.

22. "Halts 'Red' Talk at Gastonia Trial," *NYT*, October 12, 1929, 23.

23. "Halts 'Red' Talk at Gastonia Trial," *NYT*, October 12, 1929, 23; "Barnhill Bars Race Question from Evidence," *CO*, October 12, 1929, 1.

24. "Red Issue Curbed as Beal Testifies," *NYT*, October 15, 1929, 18; "Beal Claims He Hid During Shooting," *CO*, October 15, 1929, 1.

25. "Discussing the Negro" (editorial), *CO*, October 10, 1929, 8.

26. "Why They Are in Charlotte" (editorial), *CO*, October 18, 1929, 8.

27. He was elected in the summer of 1929; see "David Clark Elected Director of Rotary International," *STB*, June 13, 1929, 23.

28. “Clark Scouts Importance of Youth’s Strike at Gastonia: Publisher declares Communistic Program of Free Love and Inter-Racial Intercourse Misses Fire,” *CO*, April 6, 929, 1. The “two boys and a girl” probably are Beal, Pershing, and Vera Buch. Clark is mistaken, of course, to think that the “Young Communists” are part of the I.W.W. See also “Communists Threaten Sweeping Textile Strike,” *The Charlotte Observer*, April 5, 1929, 1; “Will Workers Stand for It?” (editorial), *CO*, April 18, 1929, 8; “Will They Accept Negroes?” (editorial), *CO*, May 14, 1929, 8.

29. “The Battle of the Grafters,” *STB*, April 18, 1929, 22.

30. “The Right of Violence,” *STB*, April 25, 1929, 30.

31. “The Negro in New York,” *STB*, July 25, 1929, 25.

32. “A McDonald and a Negro,” *STB*, August 1, 1929, 27.

33. See comments in “William Z. Foster,” *STB*, August 8, 1929, 26; “A Deplorable Situation,” *STB*, August 15, 1929, 23; “Done Said Too Damn Much,” *STB*, August 22, 1929, 22; “Nerves Do Snap,” *STB*, September 12, 1929, 30; “Communism,” *STB*, September 19, 1929, 17.

34. “What Difference?” *STB*, October 3, 1929, 24.

35. The term “black better class” is taken from Janette Thomas Greenwood’s fine study of class and race in New South Charlotte, *Bittersweet Legacy. The Black and White “Better Classes” in Charlotte, 1850-1910* (Chapel Hill: University of North Carolina Press, 1994).

36. “Let the Courts Decide,” *SofZ*, September 19, 1929, 4.

37. “Justice in North Carolina,” *SofZ*, September 12, 1929, 3.

38. Mobbing and Whipping White People,” *SofZ*, September 19, 1929, 1.

39. “Capital and Labor,” *SofZ*, August 22, 1929, 4.

7

What Is To Be Done?

Confronted by waves of labor rebellion, southern newspapers had to face, if they were to be honest to themselves and to the reality they attempted to report, some remarkably difficult questions. The answers they arrived at were complex and often surprising.

Early explanations of the troubles — that workers were plump and contented before the strikes, but were driven wild by criminal outside agitators; that the only issue at stake was the restoration of law and order; that the strikes were basically a kind of crime wave — simply didn't satisfy as mill after mill went out. Struggling to find truer, richer, deeper answers, the hometown papers increasingly found themselves exploring uncharted terrain.

Consider, for example, the papers' commentary on the relationship between the need for order and the question of labor.

There is no doubt that the forces of order — town police, the county sheriffs, the whole legal apparatus — was, in general, on the side of capital. Deputies did not rush into the streets to protect union organizers; management did not end up in the county jail. The press in full-throated chorus called all through that wild season for a restoration of law and order. Not economic justice but the restoration of order, many papers insisted again and again, was the first and only issue at hand. Yet again and again, the newspapers expressed a certain sympathy, if not for unions, at least for workers, as well as a certain irritation with the forces of order.

In every strike scene local authorities reinforced the police with hastily recruited "special deputies." These "special deputies," recruited typically from among plant guards and the more red-blooded American Legionnaires, were indeed a problem, given the volatile combination of their fervent anti-unionism and their utter lack of professional law enforcement training. In Gastonia, from the very beginning, there were constant clashes between strikers and deputies, and it seemed to some that as often as not it was the deputies who were at fault. In April, for instance, the

Charlotte News, all the while denouncing the communist agitators, wrote of the deputies, "it is in evident that those who have been left to represent the law in Gaston County in view of the withdrawal of State troops ought to be taken off to school somewhere before being put on duty and instructed in what this thing of law is all about. They don't seem to understand it exactly." The *News* thought the special deputies' handling of the most recent Gastonia strikers' march, the march in which the *Charlotte Observer*'s Legette Blythe was beaten up, ludicrous," and added, "[The deputies] appeared to be the chief offenders in the staging of another sort of a mob outbreak. Those who represent the law . . . must be lawful."[1]

The *Greensboro Daily News* was just as scathing in its comments. The paper rebuked the Gastonia special deputies for an unprovoked attack on strikers in late April and linked that attack to the vigilante raid on union headquarters earlier that month: "the whole incident throws an illuminating light on how law and order are maintained in Gastonia. It may even throw enough light on conditions there to explain to Governor Gardner, who has been reported as mystified at the masked gang outrage, something of the spirit which produces both official brutality and midnight mobbing."[2]

The southern press was unanimous in its call for fair trials for strikers in general and for the Gastonia Seven in particular. Even the fire-breathing *Gastonia Daily Gazette* called for an impartial trial of the Gastonia Reds. The *Greensboro Daily Record*'s opinion was typical: "The religious, political, and economic opinions of these defendants should have no weight with the jury in determining their guilt or innocence." It was essential that the trial be fair, the paper continued, because it wasn't only the defendants who were on trial, it was the entire legal system of North Carolina. But, the *Record* concluded, "there is every reason to believe that the trial at Charlotte will be fairly and impartially conducted and that each and every one of the defendants will find a full measure of justice."[3]

You could almost hear the southern press's collective sigh of relief when the presiding judge at the Gastonia Seven trial, Maurice V. Barnhill, proved to be, overall, skilled, professional, and fair.[4]

The fact was that southern society reacted in a host of contradictory ways to the strikes, and all these contradictions rattled through the newspaper reporting.

There were greater and lesser contradictions. For example: southern county jails were notoriously bad, but they weren't all bad. The UTW's Al Hoffmann eventually served twenty-three days in the McDowell County Jail for "rioting" in Marion. Yet upon his release in September 1930, Hoffmann, who tipped the scales at 300 pounds, joked that he had actually gained weight during his sentence.[5]

Or: though unwaveringly hostile to communists, southern politicians had at the very same time quite mixed views about trade unions. Most politicians responded to the strikes not with ideological fervor but with as much avoidance and confusion as anything else. Certainly state governors were reluctant to get involved in the dogfight between capital and labor, though in September 1929 Virginia's John

Pollard, then running for governor, actually made a rousing pro-union speech on Labor Day.[6]

Max Gardner, North Carolina's governor, approached the whole issue with very mixed feelings. A mill owner himself, Gardner was most at home in the company of corporate executives. He worried about communist subversives in his home state, yet again and again he defended publicly the right of labor, as well as capital, to organize. He denounced vigilante violence in no uncertain terms and even questioned, gingerly to be sure, the mantras of southern capital. Maybe, he thought, cheap labor wasn't the key to prosperity; maybe trade unions served a useful and legitimate function; maybe investments in the citizenry's overall quality of life, in things like education and health, were appropriate functions of the state acting for the commonwealth at large; maybe the state was not a foreign and meddlesome entity at all, but the proper if all too often bumbling expression of the will of the people; maybe there were interests in the state beyond those of organized capital.

Commenting about the trouble in Marion, in August 1929 Governor Gardner said, "The whole rhythm of America today is change and men must not think they can act to their employes or employers as they did 25 years ago." He went on, "of course, a man cannot be made to listen to his employes but he is making a grave mistake if he does not."[7]

"We cannot build a prosperous citizenship on low wages," Gardner later remarked to the *New York Times*, and that seemingly simple comment reflected a stunning intellectual revolution. Cheap labor was the key to prosperity in the South, organized capital had claimed for decades; hence the absolute need to break unions, limit social investments, and resolutely drive wages down. What Max Gardner was groping for was a way to move North Carolina and the South from a low wage, low-skill, low-tech, low value-added, economy to a high wage, high skill, high-tech, high value-added economy. If Governor Gardner were right, if, in the end, high wages, flowing from high-skilled, steady jobs performed in safe and decent workplaces — and not cheap, unskilled, and unorganized labor — were the key to a "prosperous citizenship," and if others besides him began to think this way, then a revolution of dramatic proportions was impending. Now, heaven only knew that cautious Max Gardner was no Tom Paine, but already in 1929 he was beginning to express some of the instincts of a New Deal Democrat, something potentially subversive of both the Lost Cause and the New South.

A substantial part of the southern press welcomed Gardner's comments. Even the *Gastonia Daily Gazette*, its fury cooled by August, thought that Governor Gardner's suggestions were fruitful.[8] In October, to be sure, the *Greensboro Daily News* laughed at Gardner's backpeddling away from the radical implications of his comments — the *New York Times* had reported the governor's remarks under the headline: "Urges Higher Wage in Textile Industry, North Carolina Governor Also Favors Shorter Hours, Abolition of Company Houses," and that story had gotten poor Max Gardner in very hot water with his mill owner friends. He tried to explain that, well yes, the *Times* article was, well, accurate, but the headline had exaggerated what he had really meant to say, and so on. The *Daily News*, laughed at the governor's confusion but applauded the substance of his comments.[9]

Not everyone was as coy as Max Gardner. More than anything else, it was the sight especially of all the evictions that disturbed the newspapers. Wherever a strike broke out, mill owners instinctively rushed to compliant judges who gladly issued eviction orders to workers who occupied company housing. Eviction notices in hand, nervous deputies then invaded mill homes and dragged the millhands' pitiful jumble of possessions into the street. The millhands, enraged, embarrassed, and now homeless, found themselves industrial refugees in the textile wars. More than anything else, it was all the evictions that provoked, for example, the *Raleigh News and Observer* to brood about the entire process of southern industrialization.

Narrowly and legally, of course, the paper wrote, mill management had every right to evict striking workers from company housing. The moral issue involved was wider and deeper than the legal issue, however. The sight of sheriffs invading homes and pulling people's possessions out into the street offended profoundly. "There is something about free men," the *News and Observer* editorialized, "that instinctively resents the violation of the home, that resents entry into the home even by the law. It applies to a rented home as well as to a home free from rent or mortgage." Of course, low-rent company housing was a central part of the whole mill village scheme, the paper agreed. No doubt, genuine paternal feeling did indeed inspire, on occasion, employers,

> yet it might very well be understood that the cotton mill . . . that controls the living quarters of its employes, even though it may credit itself with kindly humanitarian motives in providing cheap rental, is paying a low price for a stern control that may be and frequently is exercised relentlessly when there is occasion for the mill to exert pressure . . . company-owned housing, representing a very definite physical control over employes, may not be a cause of industrial strife, but it rarely fails to add bitterness and sometimes to afford occasion for violence.

Company-owned housing, whatever its economic logic, simply fails to contribute, the paper argued, "to the development of an independent, self-reliant, contented citizenship."

Company-owned housing, however, the paper went on, was only one part of the whole mill village system — that complex of cheap labor, union-busting, company housing, company stores, intrusive management, low-tech, low-value-added-products, bad schools, bad health-care, government-by-business-oligarchy, starved social investment, racism, and self-righteous piety that seemed to some so typical of southern life. Maybe, the *News and Observer* argued, we've gotten it all wrong. Maybe mill village paternalism actually provoked the kind of radicalism the strikes' critics so feared. "Paternalism is no insurance of industrial peace," the paper concluded, "and it is a sure breeder of enemies that go beyond the company village to attack the foundations of society itself."[10]

After the Marion killings, in October 1929, the *News and Observer* said simply: "the system is wrong."[11]

This, of course, was it exactly. Across the South mayors and judges and police chiefs and preachers and editors were groping toward some way out of the violence, realizing, as the *Greensboro Daily News* argued, that law and order could only last if questions of wages, working conditions, and workers' rights — the question of labor — were resolved justly.[12] Was labor a commodity, to be bought cheaply and used up in the production process, or was labor something more, something different? What sort of claim did workers have on the profits they, in large part, produced? Were millhands really citizens? Did they have the same rights and duties as mill owners? Did their rights as citizens — rights to free speech and free assembly — end at the mill gate? Did the South's social institutions foster, or did they eviscerate, an active and vibrant citizenry? Did they encourage human flourishing for everyone — or did they perpetuate a perverse and ultimately dysfunctional hierarchy of privilege and deference, power and powerlessness?

The strikes hurled the question of labor onto the South's front pages, and encouraged some very subversive thinking.

These dangerous thoughts were not entirely new. Even as the strike wave began, in the spring of 1929, North Carolina launched what the *Raleigh News and Observer* described as "the most liberal" workmen's compensation program in the South, and "one of the fairest in the country." Under the provisions of the new law, any North Carolina worker injured on the job could apply to the new State Industrial Commission for both medical care and financial compensation. The new workers' compensation scheme would not make anyone rich, but it would prevent disabled workers and their families from falling into poverty.[13]

At the very beginning of the strike wave, in April 1929, North Carolina's Commissioner of Labor, Frank Grist, told reporters that all the labor trouble demonstrated the crying need for new labor legislation. Grist was part of a negotiating team rushed to Forest City, North Carolina, where angry millhands had walked out of the Florence Mill to protest the stretch-out. At Grist's urging management in Forest City agreed to abandon the stretch-out, though they refused his other suggestion for an across-the-board wage hike. Grist insisted that North Carolina needed an aggressive Department of Labor, and urged the state to at least begin to compile reliable labor statistics. There was, according to the *Raleigh News and Observer*, considerable sympathy in the state assembly for legislation setting a legal limit to the maximum number of hours in the workweek, limiting night hours for women and children, and for a variety of other labor reforms.

The *News and Observer* enthusiastically championed reform in labor legislation. "It isn't too much to believe," the *N & O* editorialized in April,

> that out of the entire situation will come good for the textile worker and the cotton mills. Too long the South has been held up to dividend hungry New England cotton mill stockholders as a land of cheap labor, willing to work long hours, under conditions that would not be permitted legally in New England. Only a very poor and a very nearsighted brand of Southern patriotism can rejoice over the accession of industries from the North under such terms. Anyhow, it is time that North Carolina at least let the world know that we don't want within

our borders any industry that cannot live under enlightened labor laws. We don't want here industries that can thrive to their content only at the cost of impoverished labor and the exploitation of women and children.[14]

Some sort of consensus, embodied in legislation, regarding the rights and responsibilities of capital and labor, had to be forged, the *News and Observer* insisted. In August 1929 it listed some of the reforms it thought North Carolina needed. The specific legal rights of labor and management, especially with regard to strikes, needed to be spelled out; North Carolinians had to reach some common agreement regarding wage standards and working conditions. The rights of both labor and capital to organize and bargain collectively had to be guaranteed legally. The state needed some sort of nonpartisan arbitration board to help settle industrial disputes. "The problems of labor," the paper said, "are becoming increasingly pressing in this State. The industrialization of the State is assurance that these problems are not going to subside unless they are met squarely."[15]

Wages, of course, were on everyone's mind. Wages were already low in textiles, but after the fall of 1929, most manufacturers were convinced that there was no alternative to slashing wages even more. That, though, said the *Richmond Times-Dispatch*, was a foolish notion. Such action would do little more than turn an already poor worker into an even poorer customer and credit risk. "The immediate effect of a nation-wide reduction would be calamitous," the *Times-Dispatch* warned. What was needed at this time of economic crisis were not wage cuts but wage increases.[16]

In fact, organized capital itself debated all through 1929 the possibility of cutting hours, raising wages, and improving conditions, and all the turmoil certainly inspired such deliberations. Some improvements were, in fact, begun (though all too often quickly abandoned as the depression worsened). In August 1929, for instance, the yarn mills in Gaston county voluntarily reduced the workweek from sixty to fifty-five hours without cutting pay. In most cases the millhands were even asked how they wanted to organize the fifty-five hour shifts. The radical idea of asking workers how they preferred to work, though much discussed long before the strike wave, was obviously, according to the *Raleigh News and Observer*, hastened along by the millhands' militancy.[17] Then, in October 1930 delegates to the Cotton Textile Institute's annual convention, which represented virtually all textile manufacturers, voted overwhelmingly to eliminate night work for women and minors.[18]

Already in 1929–31, the kind of "ratcheting effect" in labor-management relations that historian Timothy Minchin has identified had begun. In order to avoid unions, management began on its own to meet some union demands. Southern textiles remained largely unorganized in part because the very threat of unions encouraged the sorts of reforms the unions advocated. A kind of indirect, informal, ongoing negotiation had always characterized labor-management relations in the mills. Although it was a thoroughly unequal negotiation — no one pretended capital ever saw labor as an equal — it was nevertheless, as Douglas Flamming argues, a dynamic process in which labor, though often unorganized, could extract some improvements. The 1929–31 strikes failed, but the workers threw the fear of labor into capital and encouraged thereby at least some of the reforms capital so often so adamantly resisted.

Public opinion in the South, at least as reflected in the media, was not anti-labor. Most papers in the southern Piedmont were appalled by the mob violence directed against union organizers. Week after week, for instance, the *Raleigh News and Observer* denounced vigilantism and noted that scores of other state newspapers shared its opinion — for instance, the *Greensboro Daily News*, the *Fayetteville Advocate*, the *Warren Record*, the *Chapel Hill Weekly*, the *Hickory Record*, and the *Shelby Star*. All these papers agreed that anti-union vigilantism was a disgrace to the old North state.[19]

Southern newspapers were unequivocally hostile to the Gastonia communists, yet most southern editors also thought the *Gastonia Daily Gazette* had gone off its rocker. The *Greensboro Daily News*, for instance, commented acidly on the flaming full-page ad in the *Gastonia Daily Gazette* entitled "Mob Rule v. Law And Order!" The *Daily News* noted that:

> References to revolution, bloodshed, blood red banner, disbelief in marriage, religion, and God, the insistence on the purported determination "to kill, kill, kill," are, of course, the natural and inevitable phraseology which accompanies the mention of "communism" . . . but what puzzles the *Daily News* is what the sort of hysteria revealed in the advertisement is going to do to . . . Gastonia?[20]

Throughout the crisis the *Greensboro Daily News* again and again called for calm, nonviolence, and open and free negotiations between labor and capital. The *Daily News* placed the blame for the Gastonia vigilantes running amok in early September squarely on the "campaign of hate" launched, it said, by the *Gastonia Daily Gazette.* [21]

The *Danville Register* warned that all the anticommunist fervor could be a threat to fundamental freedoms, particularly free speech. The *Register*, in an October 1930 editorial, reported that the Daughters of the American Revolution had recently denounced the University of Wisconsin as an "unAmerican institution" when it turned out that a Milwaukee communist was a Wisconsin alumnus. Wisconsin's President, Glenn Frank had replied, "Well what of it? We are apt to have both Communists and Presbyterians here. I have said and still say, a student has as much right to be a Communist as he has to be a Presbyterian or a Baptist. It is not the business of a university to dictate the political and religious beliefs of its students." Down in Danville the *Register* cheered. Frank, it editorialized, "struck just the right note." It was the self-anointed "professional patriots" who were the real problem, the *Register* concluded, and "it is universities like Wisconsin that defeat Communists!"[22]

Later, in January 1931, the *Register* again denounced red-baiting. The U.S. House had set up a committee, led by Representative Hamilton Fish, to investigate the communist threat to America, the *Register* reported. The Fish Committee, the *Register* snorted, did little more than drag a red herring across the trail of the genuine public policy issues. What mattered in America, the *Register* editorialized, were issues such as farm policy and unemployment, and neither had anything to do with the so-called "communist threat." The *Register* was outraged by the Fish Committee's recommendations. The committee "decides that the United States Government has reached that point in its evolution where it is necessary to place limitations on the doctrine of freedom of thought, although there is not a single Communist in the Congress of the United States, not a single Communist who is governor of a State, nor the semblance of a Communist 'threat' in politics." The *Danville Register*, yellow-dog Democratic paper that it was, clearly thought the Fish Committee's work was nothing but an effort to obscure the failures of the Hoover Administration. The *Register* thought the Committee's claims about the "Communist threat" were hogwash.[23]

The *Raleigh News and Observer*, North Carolina's self-proclaimed progressive voice, consistently ridiculed what it considered to be the *Gastonia Gazette*'s exaggerations. "Now is the time," the *News and Observer* mocked early on, "for all good patriots to look under their beds at night. The communists are coming." Of course, no one supports the Reds, said the *News and Observer*, but they are not the real problem.[24] The problem is that poor working conditions in the mills breed trouble. In fact, the *News and Observer* went on, the best way to prevent radicalism would be to encourage trade unionism. By fighting so fiercely against responsible trade unions, mill owners were only encouraging the radicals they so mightily feared. "If the radical labor element should ever get a foothold in the textile industry of the South," the *News and Observer* argued, "it will be because of the attitude of mill owners toward the efforts of the sane and conservative American Federation of labor and its textile group to organize the South."[25]

While the *Charlotte Observer* was unquestionably pro-capital and anti-labor, the *Raleigh News and Observer* vigorously defended the right of labor to organize, and the *Greensboro Daily News* more often than not blamed wooden-headed mill managers for disaffecting their workers. The Danville papers were generally anti-union, but the *Richmond Times-Dispatch* was, if not exactly pro-labor, consistently critical of Dan River Mill's autocratic manager, H. R. Fitzgerald. In fact all through the strikes, the southern press frequently turned a jaundiced eye on organized capital. At the very least, mill managers seemed woefully out of touch with their workers. "In the Gastonia affair," for instance, the *Charlotte News* thought, "it appears that the mill management was ignorant of the causes leading up to the walkout."[26] The *Charlotte News*'s opinion on labor was much more typical than that of the *Gastonia Daily Gazette*'s. On April 4, at the very beginning of the Loray strike, the *News* wrote: "Labor has just as much right to be organized as has capital or anybody else." The *News* denounced the Communists, but continued: "labor organizations of America of the saner sort and with the American imprimatur upon them have much to commend them to the intelligent public. They are as separate and distinct from the communists as the night is apart from the day."[27] The *Raleigh News and Observer* made the same point.[28]

The textile strikes of 1929–31 provoked an intense public debate among southerners about the fate of the South. Like all such debates, it was more often than not confused and messy, filled with cliches and prejudices, and often impervious to evidence. What the debate reflected was the exact opposite of a solid South. What it reflected was a white South confused, divided, fearful of communists, adamantly segregationist, often anti-union, but simultaneously sympathetic to workers, deeply worried by but also increasingly attracted to dramatic social, cultural, economic, and social change.

This debate about the fate of the South occurred not simply in state houses and colleges campuses but in a multitude of hometown papers. It was a debate, for all its faults, that included remarkable thoughtfulness and moral concern.

Consider a single example: the *Greensboro Patriot* was a weekly paper that people in Greensboro and Guilford County, North Carolina, read because it told all about who married whom and when the county fair would open. In that sense the *Greensboro Patriot* was even closer to the texture of people's lives than the bigger papers were. The *Patriot* took an active interest in the strike wave. It condemned violence no matter who the perpetrator; it vigorously repudiated the Gastonia communists.

As the strikes wore on, however, the *Patriot* began to see them as a symptom of a potentially decisive turning point in southern life. In mid-September the *Patriot* angrily condemned the culture of hysteria and vigilantism that had taken over, it claimed, in Gastonia. The *Patriot* had no sympathy for the "ravings of a small and misguided band" of millhands who had been led astray by "the lies of a band of communists." The *Patriot* thought, however, that by far the greater issue was the fact that "the mill owners have made heavy capital of the weakness of their opponents and attention has been effectively diverted for months, perhaps years, from the working conditions and living conditions which are behind the whole thing."

The *Patriot* then quoted extensively from an editorial in the *Richmond News-Leader*. The *News-Leader* editorial admirably, the *Patriot* thought, presented the most coherent understanding of the civil war in textiles. The *Patriot* reprinted the whole thing because it presented so well the complexity, and the opportunity, associated with strikes. According to the *News-Leader*:

> Gastonia is unashamed because Gastonia is uninformed . . . for Gastonia no longer thinks this a struggle between strikers and mill owners. The man who walks the streets of the Gaston county town six days in the week and goes to church on the seventh looks on the battle being fought around him as a struggle between God and the devil. The question is not one of wages, in his opinion, but one of righteousness. For he has become convinced that the strike was started and is supported by radicals who are preaching atheism, free love, racial equality and Communism, and against these things the small-town Carolinian will fight to the death. The

men who killed Mrs. Ella Wiggins did not constitute a mob in the judgement of their neighbors. They are crusaders.

Communism, in short, has taken the place of anti-evolution as the temporary bogey of the South, and it will be combatted with like passion until the people realize that the issue is not Communism but justice, not a principle of government but a principle of fair play in industry. The way to combat Communism is the simplest and the straightest — to prevent it. Communism never grows where industrial justice is done and a living wage is paid.

Does the South want to avoid the "importation of Communists"? Then let the South courageously face the reorganization of her industry on the basis of a living wage. Does the South want to be free of agitators? Fill the stomachs of Southern workers, give them decent homes in which to live, and they will not listen to agitators.

The very people who froth and talk of defending their town against radicals will themselves, in time, be the victims of the industrialism that sweats its labor. The thing is contagious. In fact, there are few men in Gastonia or in any Southern textile town today who are not suffering already from the low wages paid in the mills. No merchant keeps alive, no professional man is well paid, no independent artisan finds regular work in a town where the majority of the people make no more than enough to pay the landlord and the grocer. The measure of prosperity in any town is the margin it sets between a starvation wage and a living wage.

What is happening [in Gastonia] may happen anywhere in the South, in any underpaid industry. Instead of meeting in conventions, singing patriotic songs and pledging loyalty to American institutions in opposition to Communism, wise manufacturers should study their own payrolls and see that the wages they allow are the highest the industry can afford. This is wisdom, this is prudence, and that is patriotism.[29]

Throughout the strike wave some southern papers contented themselves with mechanical and simplistic explanations for the chaos around them. Most did not. To be sure, wisdom, prudence, and patriotism were not always consistent virtues in the southern press in the days of the strikes. Yet somehow, sometimes second hand, they were there if you looked for them, not only in the pages of the big city papers, but in the hometown papers, too, there mingled with the news about county fairs, tobacco prices, coming revivals, and pig-pickins, there in the dense, contradictory complexity of everyday small-town southern life.

NOTES

1. "Lawlessness by Law Enforcers" (editorial), *CN*, April 23, 1929, 8.

2. "How Law and Order are Maintained at Gastonia" (editorial), *GDN*, April 24, 1929, 6; also "'We Were Powerless'" (editorial), *GDR*, September 10, 1929, 4.

3. "The Trial at Charlotte" (editorial), *GDR*, August 27, 1929, 4.

4. See, for instance, the *GDG*'s call for a fair trial: "A Fair Trial" (editorial), from the *GDG*, *NO*, July 27, 1929, 4; also: "The Gastonia Case" (editorial), *RNO*, July 29, 1929, 4; "Judge Barnhill's Wisdom" (editorial), *RNO*, July 31, 1929, 4.

5. "Union Leaders Declared Guilty of Rioting Charge and Get Road Sentences," *RNO*, December 1, 1929, 1; "Strike Leader is Out of Jail," *GDR*, September 29, 1930, 1.

6. "Model Labor Day Speech" (editorial), *RNO*, September 5, 1929, 4.

7. "We Live in a New Day" (editorial), *RNO*, August 25, 1929, 4.

8. "The Heart of the Matter," from the *GDG*, in *RNO*, August 28, 1929, 4.

9. "What Governor Gardner Said" (editorial), *GDN*, October 2, 1929, 6; "The Gardner Program, in New York and in North Carolina" (editorial), *GDN*, October 3, 1929, 6.

10. "Paternalism" (editorial), *RNO*, August 18, 1929, 4.

11. "The System is Wrong" (editorial), *RNO*, October 10, 1929, 4; see also: "Wages of Textile Workers" (editorial), *RNO*, October 19, 1929, 4.

12. "Marion," from the *Greensboro News*, in *RNO*, August 22, 1929, 4.

13. "Assembly Proves Friend of Labor," *RNO*, March 24, 1929, 1; "New North Carolina Laws Become Effective Monday," *RNO*, June 30, 1929, 1.

14. "Claims Strikes Reveal Need of New Labor Law," *RNO*, April 10, 1929, 1; "Fifty-five Hour Week For Cotton Mills is Foreseen" *RNO*, April 14, 1929, 1; "As a Result of the Strike" (editorial), *RNO*, April 15, 1929, 4.

15. "Strike Against the State" (editorial), *RNO*, August 17, 1929, 4.

16. "Against Cutting Wages" (editorial), *RT-D*, August 2, 1930, 6.

17. "Mills Cut Down Hours of Work," *RNO*, August 10, 1929, 1; "Shorter Hours" (editorial), *RNO*, August 10, 1929, 4.

18. "Women Voted Better Hours in Textile Plants," *RTD*, October 16, 1930, 1.

19. See, for instance, "And We Learn About Reds from Them" (editorial), *RNO*, April 19, 1929, 4; "North Carolina Looks to the Governor" (editorial), *RNO*, April 21, 1929, 4; "The State and the Mob," from the *Greensboro Daily News*, *RNO*, April 22, 1929, 4; "Action and Quick Action" (editorial), *RNO*, April 23, 1929, 4; "Gastonia's High Duty" (editorial), *RNO*, April 25, 1929, 4; "Justice and Only Justice" (editorial), *RNO*, April 26, 1929, 4; "The Record Thus Far," from the *Greensboro News*, *RNO*, April 26, 1929, 4; "The Gastonia Outrage," from the *Fayetteville Advocate*, *RNO*, April 27, 1929, 4; "A Challenge," from the *Warren Record*, *RNO*, April 27, 1929, 4; "A Disgrace" from the *Chapel Hill Weekly*, *RNO*, April 28, 1929, 4; "Mob Against Mob," from the *Hickory Record*, *RNO*, April 29, 1929, 4; "Should Run Them Down," from the *Shelby Star*, *RNO*, April 29, 1929, 4.

20. "Two Exhibits" (editorial), *GDN*, April 6, 1929, 6.

21. See, for instance, "The State and the Mob" (editorial), *GDN*, April 20, 1929, 6; "Sitting Quietly and Calmly" (editorial), *GDN*, April 21, 1929, 6; "It Demands Action," *GDN*, April 23, 1929, 6; "The Natural Result of Campaigns of Hate" (editorial), *GDN*, September 11, 1929, 6.

22. "Nonchalance and Communism" (editorial), *DR*, October 31, 1930, 4.

23. "The Fish (Red Herring) Trail" (editorial), *DR*, January 20, 1931, 4.

24. "The Communist Bugagoo," *RNO*, April 6, 1929, 4.

25. "Fuel to the Fire" (editorial), *RNO*, April 5, 1929, 4; see also: "Somebody Call a Cop!" (editorial), *RNO*, April 7, 1929, 4.

26. "Everybody Loses in a Strike," *CN*, April 5, 1929, 8.

27. "Disorders in Textile Plants" (editorial), *CN*, April 4, 1929, 8.

28. "The State Federation of Labor" (editorial), *RNO*, August 13, 1929, 4.

29. "Gastonia is Unashamed" (editorial), *GP*, September 19, 1929, 4. In later editorials, the *Patriot* would reject the obsession with cheap labor as "suicidal," and urge manufacturers to work closely with the AFL trade-unions. See for example, "A Fair Trial for The Strikers"

(editorial), *GP*, September 30, 1929, 4; "The Drive for Unionization" (editorial), *GP*, October 7, 1929, 4.

Conclusion: "Journalism Below the Potomac"

In 1926 a talented young North Carolina journalist named Gerald Johnson published a scathing attack on southern journalism in H. L. Mencken's *American Mercury.* Johnson's article, filled with Menckenesque mockery, was called "Journalism Below the Potomac."[1] Southern journalism, Johnson wrote, is now "near to perfection." Advertising sales were booming, publishers were flush with cash, newspaper editors (though not reporters), had become Respectable Citizens in their hometowns: "the typical newspaper man of the New South has an aldermanic paunch and a multiplicity of chins. . . . His taste in cigars is apt to be as fastidious as that of a Wall Street operator. His bootlegger is the one who caters to the mayor. He submits to the revilings of the pro at the golf club as meekly as do the presidents of the First National Bank and the spinning-mills."[2]

Newspapermen had become Businessmen, Johnson continued, and as such they had become representatives of wealth and not the commonwealth. As Businessmen, editors' interests neatly merged with those of the powers that be, those courthouse cliques of textile mill owners, lawyers, bankers, and politicians, and so their newspapers became not tribunes of the people but propagandists for the rulers. Nothing quite so crude as censorship occurs, Johnson admitted. In fact, he argued, something even worse operated, self-censorship. The southern editor "realizes as keenly as any realtor that the first duty of a Business Man is never to knock the town" For instance, " if the cotton-mill hands strike, nobody has to tell the newspaper proprietor what to do. . . . All his higher instincts persuade him that nobody but a foreign agitator paid with Soviet gold could have persuaded the mill-hands that the right length of a working day is ten hours instead of the eleven hallowed by tradition."[3]

To be sure, he asserted, this was not all the editors' fault. Editors do indeed respond to public demand, and so far the southern public had been gentle in its demands. The southern public is content with the grist of the Associated Press dispatches in the news columns. It is content with an editorial page made up of thundering denunciations of the Republican party and of Antichrist, variously personified in Clarence Darrow, the Pope, Harry Emerson Fosdick and the Elders of Zion, balanced by maudlin eulogies of the Southern climate, the Confederacy, cotton manufacturers, and successful realtors.[4]

On the other hand, in Johnson's opinion, there were some signs of light in this pervasive grey. Some newspapers had freed themselves of the local elites and had begun to act as representatives not of the interests but of the people. Some have even dared to be more than passive reflectors of passing public moods, and had tried to inform, provoke, and heighten public awareness. Some had tried to offer their readers something beyond cliche, stereotype, and diversion. Some had actually dared to be original, thought-provoking, and critical. Johnson praised the *Greensboro Daily News*, edited by Earle Godbey; Julian Harris's *Columbus* (Georgia) *Enquirer-Sun*; Laurence Stalling's *Macon* (Georgia) *Telegraph*; Josephus Daniels' *Raleigh News and Observer*; and a few others. They were though, Johnson thought, exceptions. Although he obviously hoped for a change, he clearly was deeply critical of the southern papers. Journalism below the Potomac was a sorry business at best.

Johnson, of course, had ample reason for pessimism. The truth, though, was more complex than Johnson's brief satire would suggest. Certainly the majority of southern newspapers thought of themselves first and foremost as hometown boomers, and that, in turn, meant unfailing fidelity to business and unquestioning support of the South's apartheid society and plutocratic politics. Southern papers were defenders of the way things were and the powers that be.

The *Charlotte Observer*, for example, liked to think of itself as the "*New York Times* of the South," and as early as the turn of the century, the *Observer* was recognized as one of the South's premiere papers.[5] From its founding just after the Civil War, well into the 1930s and beyond, the *Observer* was both ideologically and personally tied to the New South's leading business interests. The paper's early owners included D. A. Tompkins, one of the South's leading entrepreneurs. In the late nineteenth century, the *Observer* helped organize the Southern Manufacturers' Club. It was unshakably anti-union, anti-Populist, anti-social reform and pro-business, pro-segregation, and pro-Democratic party. From its origins it was proud to be the "business voice of the Piedmont."[6] During the strike wave of 1929–31, it was relentlessly anticommunist, and more often than not anti-union.

It would be a mistake, however, to overlook the complexities in the *Observer*'s position.

For example, it was in October 1929 that the *New York Times* glowingly praised North Carolina's Governor, Max Gardner, so glowingly, in fact, that Governor Gardner had to explain to his cotton mill-owner friends that he wasn't really that much of a reformer. According to the *Times*, the Governor had said: "we do not want general content . . . with our industrial or economic arrangements. We do not want complacency or smug satisfaction. We do not want docile citizens or docile employees. What we want is orderly, restrained struggle for change . . . freedom in which ideas and opinions may be advanced." The *Times* responded:

> The last hope of agitators to make it appear that textile labor in North Carolina is engaged in a struggle against the despotism of the governing class is removed by the calm and wise statement of Governor O. Max Gardner. So long as men of his type are in office workers can be certain not only of justice but of a sympathetic and intelligent insight into their grievances.

North Carolina, the *Times* concluded, was making the painful transition from agriculture to industry and experiencing all the same tensions other regions had experienced. With ideas like Governor Gardner's, however, ideas "as progressive as social workers and economists could ask," the prospect was bright.[7] Later that month, in fact, the Governor had even insisted that "labor has a right to organize. . . . They have a right to combine their efforts to combat unnecessary evil conditions."[8] This was the reporting that had gotten Governor Gardner in such hot water with his mill-owner friends, much to the amusement of North Carolina's press.

Well. What would the *Charlotte Observer* think of all this?

Surprisingly, the *Observer* cautiously endorsed the governor's position. A number of "progressive" mill owners, it wrote, had already begun to think of ways to improve the working conditions that had contributed to all the trouble. A number of mills had already moved from a sixty hour to a fifty-five hour week, without cutting pay. The *Observer* thought this all to the good:

> It would be but a hastening of a situation that is bound to come sooner or later because those of the mill people, freed from trouble as a result of the advanced stand taken toward their labor, will not be content with the situation until all mills come up to the standard they have set, to the permanent forfending against other labor troubles in this state. The backward ills must be brought forward to better hours, better wages, and better conditions.[9]

What one sees when reading through the old newspapers, in fact, is not so much the rigidity and predictability of the papers' positions, but rather the perplexities, contradictions, and downright confusions that leap from their pages. Yes indeed, Gerald Johnson's Babbitt-edited booster press did exist, but faced with textile crisis of 1929–31, the press revealed itself to be something more.

W. J. Cash, another young reporter deeply impressed by H. L. Mencken, wrote in a 1929 article for Mencken called "The Mind of the South," which would be the basis for Cash's later, famous book of the same name, that "undeniably, there is a stir, a rustling upon the land, a vague, formless intangible thing which may or may not be the adumbration of coming upheaval. Tomorrow — the day after — eventually — the cotton mill peon will acquire the labor outlook and explosion will follow."[10] It would be an exaggeration to say that the labor explosion of 1929–31 in any sense transformed the South; in that sense, Cash was wrong. Yet Cash was also right. The trouble in textiles forced southerners to reconsider, rethink, and redefine the textile industry and, in doing so, themselves. Changes were neither instant nor sweeping, yet they were also inexorable. The strikes of 1929–31 were an important point in the turbulent and violent process by which the South changed its mind.

The strikes were also a crucial moment in the newspapers' identities. The acid test of the strikes triggered serious reconsideration of the old alliance between the media and the mill baron elite.

In September 1930, for example, when the Danville strike began, the *Danville Register* published a long editorial calling for the city, both its citizens and its government, to be "strictly neutral" in the fight between labor and capital. On the one hand, one might view such a call as the depth of hypocrisy. There was little doubt that the *Register* itself was deeply sympathetic to capital. Moreover, if the fight was, as the union claimed, a fight for elementary justice for workers, then calls for neutrality in such a fight for justice were morally repugnant.

The editorial was more than mere cant however. It praised the orderly behavior of the trade unionists. It insisted that both sides get "fair play." It argued that the city had to protect both "the human and constitutional rights of the workers" and "the legal and property rights of the stockholders." It called for Danville to muster the "courage to be honest and just and calm." [11]

Consider also the *Richmond Times-Dispatch*'s commentary on federal unemployment relief, written in December 1930 in the midst of the Danville strike.

The *Times-Dispatch* had consistently called for federal action to combat the mass unemployment triggered by the Depression, but the paper's critics charged that such governmental action was nothing less than "communism." In response the paper ironically noted that the very people terrified by state action to help the poor are often the most vigorous defenders of state action to push their own agenda, such as nationally mandated prohibition. More important than this logical inconsistency, the *Times-Dispatch* argued, critics failed to understand that in a democracy, the democratic state is the representative of the community, and that the community needs to act in times of emergency. Of course, the paper agreed, "this country is committed to a capitalistic order. But when capitalism . . . become[s] unruly, then who, if not the Federal Government, is going to guarantee the rights and privileges of the less powerful?" A worker, the editorial continued, "has a right to have a chicken in his pot; and the Government is obligated not to see that one is put there but to see that the capitalist employer does not mismanage his affairs to such an extent that the worker is not even given the chance to buy the chicken."

Government, the paper concluded, "must protect two general groups of individuals, to side with one is to encourage a plutocracy, to side with the other is to fall into socialism, even communism." But, "so long as the . . . protection of the rights of the poor (and poor in a capitalistic society means less powerful) is the motive behind Federal legislation, then there will be no evidence of socialism."[12]

Clearly the *Times-Dispatch* was not just talking about the government's duties. The media, the paper claimed, had to steer between "plutocracy" and "communism." That it would get too close to "communism" was highly unlikely.

That it would be a court fool of the "plutocracy" was the graver danger. Significantly, what was at stake was not simply economics, not just unemployment relief or welfare. As the *Times-Dispatch* noted in its striking parenthesis, "poor in a capitalistic society means less powerful." What was at stake then, in this rethinking about the state and democracy and by implication the media too, was power, the power to shape, as Frank Porter Graham said, the kind of commonwealth we want to be.

Jack Claiborne, in summarizing the *Charlotte Observer*'s biography, writes:

> Slowly, painfully, the *Observer* . . . struggled to free itself from a repressive political party that demanded absolute loyalty. Later, it struggled again to throw off the oppressive influence of a business community that overweighted the paper's judgement and compromised its objectivity. In time, it developed a social conscience and learned to stand above the marketplace and comment honestly on the forces that were shaping life in Charlotte and the Carolinas.[13]

Virtually every paper examined here went through the same complicated and often confused process. Virtually every paper tried to distinguish among market and democracy, human rights and the rights of property, among the way things were and the way things ought to be. Slowly and often painfully, as Claiborne says, the *Observer*, the *Register*, and all their sister papers began to think of themselves as autonomous voices whose primary virtues were courage, calm, and honesty, who slowly began to think of themselves as voices of the democratic community. Heaven knows they more often than not failed to live up to those ideals, but that they increasingly held such ideals marked a watershed in their identities and social roles. Times do change and so do newspapers. The deeply conservative and often antidemocratic *Charlotte Observer* had become, by the 1990s, one of the advocates of the new "public journalism," which sees journalism not simply as a "neutral bystander" but rather as a central player in the creation and preservation of a strong, well-informed, vibrant democracy.[14]

In 1922, in *The Public Opinion*, Walter Lippmann wrote that "the facts we see depend on where we are placed and the habits of our eyes." He is not arguing for some sort of radical subjectivism; there are indeed facts to be seen. Seeing is governed, however, both by external contexts, "where we are placed," and internal preconceptions, "the habits of our eyes."[15] Both can change. The pre-depression crisis in southern textiles dramatically, if temporarily, changed the social contexts within which southerners lived. The crisis changed too the habits of their eyes.

It is in the hometown papers of the era, especially those most closely connected to the strikes, that we can see these changes. Together with the intellectuals and politicians and the social reformers, it was the editors and reporters of the hometown press, ink-stained, chain-smoking, and hard-drinking as more than a few were, who interrogated and reinterpreted and reconstructed their world. In their workaday reporting, in their hastily scribbled editorials, we can see, messily, contradictorily, sometimes incoherently, but just as often diligently and sometimes even progressively, the "mind of the South" at work.

NOTES

1. Gerald Johnson, "Journalism Below the Potomac," in Gerald Johnson, *South Watching. Selected Essays*, edited by Fred Hobson (Chapel Hill: UNC Press, 1983), 72–81.

2. Johnson, "Journalism," 72.

3. Johnson, "Journalism," 75.

4. Johnson, "Journalism," 80.

5. See Claiborne, *Observer*, 193; for comments by other newspapers on the *Observer*, see 85, 100, 112.

6. Claiborne, *Observer*, 10.

7. "Order and Progress" (editorial), *NYT*, October 1, 1929, 30.

8. "South Sees Young As Democratic Hope," *NYT*, October 20, 1929, III, 2.

9. "Taking Counsel" (editorial), *CO*, September 22, 1929, 8; "Gardner's Policies" (editorial), *CO*, October 2, 1929, 8.

10. W. J. Cash, "The Mind of the South," *American Mercury* XVII (1929), 310–18. See also Cash's article specifically on the strikes, "The War in the South," *American Mercury* XIX (1930), 163–69. Both are reprinted in Joseph Morrison, *W. J. Cash: Southern Prophet* (New York: Knopf, 1967). See also the commentary on the articles in Bruce Clayton, *W. J. Cash* (Baton Rouge: Louisiana University Press, 1991), 79ff.

11. "Preserving Neutrality in a Strike," *DR*, September 30, 1930, 4.

12. "Keeping Speech Free," *RT-D*, December 3, 1930, 8.

13. Claiborne, *Observer*, 11.

14. See Fallows' remarks about the *Charlotte Observer* in his *Breaking News*, 255.

15. Cited in Gans, *News*, 310.

Bibliography

Note: The "New South" was a media invention. Henry Grady and his Atlanta *Weekly Constitution* expressed and tirelessly promoted, if they didn't exactly single-handedly invent, the "New South." The *Constitution*'s influence was enormous. As historian Edward Ayers writes:

> By the late 1880s, Henry Grady's Atlanta *Weekly Constitution* went to every post office in Georgia and to every state in the nation, giving it the largest circulation of a weekly paper in the United States. Not only did the paper send out up to 20,000 sample copies every week, but it also employed agents who carried word and promotional materials far and wide. . . . The entire family seized on the *Constitution* as soon as it arrived each Saturday in Hatchett Creek, Alabama. Mitchell Garrett recalled how the children looked for Uncle Remus stories while their father pored over the political news and their mother read the paper aloud to entertain the family. Little of the paper went unread. (Ayers, *Promise*, 87)

Hundreds of smaller papers across the South became so many mini-*Constitutions*, indefatigably promoting the "New South" and profoundly shaping their communities.

The press had a tremendous impact on the "New South," and yet, oddly enough, the southern press is virtually unknown territory. To be sure, virtually every historian of the American South uses the press as a primary source, but studies of the press itself are remarkably rare. As the Introduction explains, there are indeed some fine histories of individual southern newspapers, such as Jack Claiborne's *The Charlotte Observer: Its Time and Place, 1869–1986* and Thomas Harrison Baker's *The Memphis "Commercial Appeal": The History of a Southern Newspaper*. There are as well studies of individual reporters and editors, such as Raymond Nixon's *Henry W. Grady: Spokesman of the New South*, Joseph Morrison's *Josephus Daniels Speaks* and John Kneebone's *Southern Liberal Journalists and the Question of Race, 1920–1944*. Solid monographs devoted to the southern press, however, are thin on the ground.

The archival material listed below provides important background information regarding the events the papers reported, but there is little archival material on the southern press itself, at least from the 1920s. What internal records newspapers might have generated have long since disappeared and few if any have found their way into archives. The papers of a handful of prominent editors have survived, but virtually nothing remains from the private lives of the working reporters. Oddly enough, journalism, one of the most public of all professions, remains difficult to approach. On the other hand, the newspapers themselves have by and large survived, at least on microfilm. Complete runs of major papers like the *Charlotte Observer*, the *Raleigh News and Observer*, the *Richmond News-Leader*, and the *Richmond Times-Dispatch* are easy to find. Just as interesting, although a little trickier to find, are the small-town papers, such as the *Gastonia Daily Gazette*, the *Elizabethton Star*, or the *Greensboro Patriot*. Often, though, they still lurk in local public libraries, and they provide particularly arresting images of daily life. The papers themselves, then, are the primary texts for this project. They are not simply sources of information about people and events beyond themselves, but are, instead, treated as structures of imagination and discourse that merit investigation on their own.

MANUSCRIPT COLLECTIONS

Danville, Virginia, Public Library

Clippings, indexed by Clara G. Fountain.
Dan River Mills File.
Schoolfield File.
Winding Through Time. Danville Bicentennial Committee Brochure, 1993.

Duke University, Durham, North Carolina, William R. Perkins Library, Manuscript Department

Boyd Ellsworth Payton Papers.
Engdahl, J. Louis. *Gastonia – A Class Case and a Class Verdict.* International Labor Defense flyer, undated.
George Sinclair Mitchell Papers.
"Stand Behind the 23 Militant Gastonia Textile Workers!" San Francisco Joint Defense and Relief Committee flyer, undated.
"Marion – Food and Clothing for 175 Families Needed!" Federal Council of Churches flyer, undated.

Gastonia, North Carolina, Gaston County Public Library

Gaston County Centennial Brochure (1846–1946). Gaston County Centennial Committed, undated.

Georgia State University, Southern Labor Archives

Pamphlets

Blanshard, Paul. *Labor in Southern Cotton Mills.*
Conference for Progressive Labor Action, *The Marion Murder.*
Lewis, Sinclair. *Cheap and Contented Labor.*
Lloyd, Jesse. *Gastonia.*
Page, Myra. *Southern Cotton Mills and Labor.*

Marion, North Carolina, McDowell County Public Library

Burleson, Debra. "The Strike of 1929 in McDowell County." Unpublished paper, undated.
Cross Mill Records.

Raleigh, North Carolina, North Carolina State Department of Cultural Resources, Division of Archives and History

Governor O. Max Gardner Papers.
Gertrude Weil Papers.
Frank Porter Graham Papers.
Robin B. Hood Collection.

University of North Carolina at Chapel Hill, Louis R. Wilson Library, Southern Historical Collection

Frank Porter Graham Papers.
Harriet Herring Papers.
Robert Cooke Papers.
William Greene Raoul Papers.

University of North Carolina at Chapel Hill, Southern Oral History Project

Interviews:

Harry and Janie Adams, by Allen Tullos, 1979.
Mildred Andrews, by Mary Murphy and Jim Leloudis, 1979.
Mary and Roy Auton, by Jacquelyn Hall, 1980.
Mareda Cobb and Carrie Yelton, by Jacquelyn Hall and Patty Dilley, 1979.
Lloyd and Betty Davidson, by Allen Tullos, 1979.
Tessie and George Dyer, by LuAnn Jones, 1980.
Alice Evitt, by Jim Leloudis, 1979.
Sam and Vesta Finley, by Mary Frederickson and Marion Roydhouse, 1975.
Carrie Gerringer, by Douglas DeNatalo, 1979.
James and Pauline Griffith, by Allen Tullos, 1979.

Lois MacDonald, by Marion Roydhouse, 1975.
Lois MacDonald, by Mary Frederickson, 1977.
Leota Lowery, by Mary Murphy, 1979.
Hoyle McCorkle, by Jim Leloudis, 1979.
Ada Wilson, by Allen Tullos, 1980.

Washington, D. C. National Archives

Labor Conciliation Service Records.

NEWSPAPERS AND MAGAZINES

American Mercury
Charlotte News
Charlotte Observer
Danville Register
Daily Worker
Elizabethton Star
Gastonia Daily Gazette
Greensboro Daily News
Greensboro Patriot
Greensboro Record
Literary Digest
Mecklenburg Times
Marion Progress
Nation
New Republic
New York Times
Raleigh News and Observer
Richmond News-Leader
Richmond Times-Dispatch
Star of Zion

BOOKS, ARTICLES, DISSERTATIONS

Aaron, Daniel. *Writers on the Left.* New York: Columbia University Press, 1992.
Alexander, Will, et al. *The Collapse of Cotton Tenancy.* Chapel Hill: University of North Carolina Press, 1935.
Anderson, Eric. *Race and Politics in North Carolina, 1872–1901. The Black Second.* Baton Rouge: Louisiana State University Press, 1981.
Anderson, Sherwood. *Beyond Desire.* New York: Horace Liveright, 1932.
Ashby, Warren. *Frank Porter Graham, Southern Liberal.* Winston-Salem: Blair, 1980.
Ayers, Edward. *The Promise of the New South.* New York: Oxford University Press, 1992.
Baker, Thomas Harrison. *The Memphis "Commercial Appeal": The History of a Southern Newspaper.* Baton Rouge: Louisiana State University Press, 1971.
Beal, Fred. *Proletarian Journey.* New York: Hillman-Curl, 1937.

Beardsley, Edward. *A History of Neglect. Health Care for Blacks and Mill Workers in the Twentieth Century.* Knoxville: University of Tennessee Press, 1987.
Berglund, Abraham, et al. *Labor in the Industrial South.* Charlottesville: University of Virginia Press, 1930.
Billings, Dwight. *Planters and the Making of a "New South": Class, Politics and Development in North Carolina, 1865–1900.* Chapel Hill: University of North Carolina Press, 1979.
Bogardus, Ralph F. and Fred Hobson, ed. *Literature at the Barricades: The American Writer in the 1930s.* Tuscaloosa: University of Alabama Press, 1982.
Boles, John and Evelyn Thomas Nelson, ed. *Interpreting Southern History.* Baton Rouge: Louisiana State University Press, 1987.
Brooks, Robert. *The United Textile Workers of America.* Ph. D. Dissertation, Yale University, 1935.
Buch, Vera. *A Radical Life.* Bloomington: Indiana University Press, 1977.
Burke, Fielding. *Call Home the Heart.* New York: Feminist Press, 1983.
Byerly, Victoria. *Hard Times and Cotton Mill Girls.* Ithaca: ILR Press, 1986.
Carleton, David. *Mill and Town in South Carolina, 1880–1920.* Baton Rouge: Louisiana State University Press, 1982.
Cash, W. J. "The Mind of the South." *American Mercury* 17 (1929), 310–18.
_____. *The Mind of the South.* New York: Vintage, 1941.
Claiborne, Jack. *The Charlotte Observer: Its Time and Place, 1869–1986.* Chapel Hill: University of North Carolina Press, 1992.
Clayton, Bruce. *W. J. Cash.* Baton Rouge: Louisiana State University Press, 1991.
Cobb, James C. *Industrialization and Southern Society, 1877–1984.* Lexington: University of Kentucky Press, 1984.
Cope, Robert and Manly Wade Wellman. *The County of Gaston.* Gastonia: Gaston County Historical Society, 1961.
Corbin, David Alan. *Life, Work, and Rebellion in the Coal Fields.* Urbana: University of Illinois Press, 1981.
Dabney, Virginius. *Virginia.* New York: Doubleday, 1971.
Daniel, Pete. *Standing at the Crossroads. Southern Life in the Twentieth Century.* New York: Hill and Wang, 1986.
Denning, Michael. *The Cultural Front.* New York: Verso: 1996.
Draper, Theodore. "Gastonia Revisited." *Social Research* 38 (Spring 1971) 1: 3–29.
Dunne, William. *Gastonia—Citadel of the Class Struggle.* New York: Workers' Library, 1929.
Dykeman, Wilma. *Tennessee. A Bicentennial History.* New York: Norton, 1975.
Earle, John, et al. *Spindles and Spires.* Atlanta: John Knox, 1976.
Egerton, John. *Speak Now Against the Day.* New York: Knopf, 1994.
Eller, Ronald. *Miners, Millhands, and Mountaineers.* Knoxville: University of Tennessee, 1982.
Escott, Paul D. *Many Excellent People. Power and Privilege in North Carolina, 1850–1900.* Chapel Hill: University of North Carolina Press, 1985.
Escott, Paul D. and David R. Goldfield, ed. *Major Problems in the History of the American South.* New York: Heath, 1990.
Fallows, James. *Breaking News: How the Media Undermine American Democracy.* New York: Vintage, 1997.

Fink, Gary. *The Fulton Bag and Cotton Mills Strike of 1914–1915.* Ithaca: ILR Press, 1993.

Flamming, Douglas. *Creating the Modern South. Millhands and Managers in Dalton, Georgia, 1884–1994.* Chapel Hill: University of North Carolina Press, 1992.

Foner, Philip. *History of the Labor Movement in the United States*, vol. 10. New York: International Publishers, 1995.

Foster, Gaines M. *Ghosts of the Confederacy. Defeat, the Lost Cause, and the Emergence of the New South.* New York: Oxford University Press, 1987.

Gans, Herbert. *Deciding What's News.* New York: Vintage, 1980.

Gaston, Paul. *The New South Creed.* New York: Vintage, 1973.

Grantham, Dewey. *The South in Modern America.* New York: Harper Collins, 1986.

Greenwald, Maurine Weiner. *Women, War, and Work.* Ithaca: Cornell University Press, 1980.

Greenwood, Janette Thomas. *Bittersweet Legacy. The Black and White "Better Classes" in Charlotte, 1850–1910.* Chapel Hill: University of North Carolina Press, 1994.

Griffin, Larry and Don Doyle. *The South as an American Problem.* Athens: University of Georgia Press, 1995.

Hagan, Jane. *The Story of Danville.* New York: Stratford House, 1950.

Hairston, L. Beatrice. *A Brief History of Danville, Virginia, 1728–1954.* Richmond: Dietz Press, 1955.

Hall, Jacquelyn Dowd. "Disorderly Women: Gender and Labor Militancy in the Appalachian South." *Journal of American History* 73 (September 1986), 354– 82.

_____, et al. *Like a Family.* Chapel Hill: University of North Carolina Press, 1987.

Hays, Arthur Garfield. *Trial by Prejudice.* Westport, Connecticut: Negro University Press, 1970.

Herring, Harriet. *Welfare Work in Mill Villages.* Chapel Hill: University of North Carolina Press, 1929.

_____. *The Passing of the Mill Villages.* Chapel Hill: University of North Carolina Press, 1949.

Hobbs, Samuel Huntington. *North Carolina: Economic and Social.* Chapel Hill: University of North Carolina Press, 1930.

Hobson, Fred. *Serpent in Eden. H. L. Mencken and the South.* Baton Rouge: Louisiana State University Press, 1974.

Hodges, James. "Challenge to the New South: The Great Textile Strike in Elizabethton, Tennessee, 1929." *Tennessee Historical Quarterly* 23 (December 1964), 343–57.

Holly, John Fred. *Elizabethton, Tennessee. A Case Study of Southern Industrialization.* Ph.D. Dissertation, Clark University, 1949.

Howie, Sam Watson. *The New South in the North Carolina Foothills. A Study of the Early Industrial Experience in McDowell County.* Master's Thesis, Appalachian State University, 1976.

Johnson, Gerald. *South Watching. Selected Essays.* Edited by Fred Hobson. Chapel Hill: University of North Carolina Press, 1983.

Kane, Nancy Frances. *Textiles in Transition. Technology, Wages, and Industry Relocation in the U.S. Textile Industry.* Westport, Connecticut: Greenwood Press, 1988.

Key, V. O. *Southern Politics in State and Nation.* Knoxville: University of Tennessee Press, 1977.

Kneebone, John. *Southern Liberal Journalists and the Question of Race, 1920–1944.* Chapel Hill: University of North Carolina Press, 1986.

Lahne, Herbert J. *The Cotton Mill Worker.* New York: Farrar and Rinehart, 1944.

Lefler, Hugh Talmage and Albert Ray Newsome. *North Carolina. A History of a Southern State.* Chapel Hill: University of North Carolina Press, 1973.

Lumpkin, Grace. *To Make My Bread.* New York: Macauley, 1932.

McCartin, Joseph. *Labor's Great War. The Struggle for Industrial Democracy and the Origins of Modern labor Relations, 1919–1921.* Chapel Hill: University of North Press, 1997.

McHugh, Cathy L. *Mill Family. The Labor System in the Southern Cotton Textile Industry, 1880–1915.* New York: Oxford University Press, 1988.

McLaurin, Melton. *Paternalism and Protest. Southern Cotton Mill Workers and Organized Labor, 1875–1905.* Westport, Connecticut: Greenwood Press, 1971.

Merritt, Davis. *Public Journalism and Public Life. Why Telling the News is Not Enough.* Hillsdale, New Jersey: Lawrence Erlbaum, 1995.

Mindich, David. *Just the Facts. How "Objectivity" Came to Define American Journalism.* New York: New York University Press, 1998.

Mitchell, Broadus. *The Rise of Cotton Mills in the South.* Baltimore: Johns Hopkins University Press, 1921.

Mitchell, George S. *Textile Unionism and the South.* Chapel Hill: University of North Carolina Press, 1931.

Montgomery, David. *Citizen Worker.* New York: Cambridge University Press, 1993.

Morrison, Joseph. *Josephus Daniels Speaks.* Chapel Hill: University of North Carolina Press, 1962.

_____. *W. J. Cash: Southern Prophet.* New York: Knopf, 1967.

Murchison, Claudius T. *King Cotton is Sick.* Chapel Hill: University of North Carolina Press, 1930.

National Organization of Women, Charlotte Chapter. *Let's Stand Together. The Story of Ella Mae Wiggins.* Charlotte: National Organization of Women, 1979.

Newby, I. A. *Plain Folk in the New South.* Baton Rouge: Louisiana State University Press, 1989.

Nixon, Raymond. *Henry W. Grady: Spokesman of the New South.* New York: Alfred Knopf, 1943.

O'Connor, Adrian. *River City. Stories of Danville.* Danville: Danville Register, 1993.

Page, Dorothy Myra. *Gathering Storm.* New York: International Publishers, 1932.

Pope, Liston. *Millhands and Preachers.* New Haven: Yale University Press, 1942.

Potwin, Marjorie. *Cotton Mill People of the Piedmont. A Study in Social Change.* New York: Columbia University Press, 1927.

Powell, William. *North Carolina Through Four Centuries.* Chapel Hill: University of North Carolina Press, 1989.

Rideout, Walter. *The Radical Novel in the United States, 1900 – 1954.* New York: Columbia University Press, 1992.

Rollins, William. *The Shadow Before.* New York: McBride, 1934.

Rubin, Louis D. *Virginia: A History.* New York: Doubleday, 1971.

Salmond, John. *Gastonia, 1929.* Chapel Hill: University of North Carolina Press, 1996.

Siegel, Frederick. *The Roots of Southern Distinctiveness. Tobacco and Society in Danville, Virginia, 1780–1865.* Chapel Hill: University of North Carolina Press, 1987.

Terrill, Tom, and Jerrold Hirsch. *Such As Us: Southern Voices of the Thirties.* Chapel Hill: University of North Carolina Press, 1978.

Tindall, George. *The Emergence of the New South.* Baton Rouge: Louisiana State University Press, 1967.

Tippett, Tom. *When Southern Labor Stirs.* New York: Cape and Smith, 1931.

_____. *Mill Shadows.* Katohah: Brookwood Labor College, 1932.

Tullos, Allen. *Habits of Industry.* Chapel Hill: University of North Carolina Press, 1989.

U. S. Senate. 71st Congress. *Report by the Committee on Manufactures,* May 8, 9, 20, Washington, D. C.: Government Printing Office, 1929.

Vorse, Mary Heaton. *Strike!* Urbana: University of Illinois, 1991.

Whalen, Robert W. "Recollecting the Cotton Mill Wars: Proletarian Literature of the 1929–1931 Southern Textile Strikes." *The North Carolina Historical Review* 75 (October 1998) 4: 370–97.

Wheeler, Marjorie Spruil. *New Women in the New South.* New York: Oxford University Press, 1993.

Williams, Robert. *The Thirteenth Juror.* Lawndale, North Carolina: Rainbow Books, 1977.

Woodward, C. Vann. *The Origins of the New South.* Baton Rouge: Louisiana State University Press, 1951.

Wright, Gavin. *Old South, New South.* New York: Basic Books, 1986.

Zieger, Robert, ed. *Organized Labor in the Twentieth-Century South.* Knoxville: University of Tennessee Press, 1991.

Index

About the Author

ROBERT WELDON WHALEN is Professor of History at Queens College in Charlotte, North Carolina.